Communities developing for health

A special report for
the Regional Director
of Public Health for
North West England
2000

Edited by Pam Ashton
and Andrew Hobbs

ISBN 0 9539574 0 3

Contents

Part 4
Communities and development

Part 5
Identifying and mobilising community skills and assets

Part 6
The way ahead

PART ONE

Introduction

Communities developing for health

When the previous Chief Medical Officer, Sir Kenneth Calman, was making one of his periodic visits to the North West Region, he began the day with a walk from the Trans-Pennine Trail in Reddish Vale, which led to a housing estate on the edge of Stockport. There the CMO was in his element, meeting residents of a housing co-operative and users of a community centre, drinking tea and chatting. The remainder of the day's programme progressed through visits to health centres and other health care facilities, finishing in a specialist tertiary centre of clinical excellence.

During the afternoon one senior medical consultant commented that he thought Sir Kenneth must have had a most interesting day but that he couldn't understand what the CMO was doing going on a walk through a housing estate! When the day was over the CMO said to me that we needed to have a conference on community development and health, to give this important field a platform and to encourage the dissemination of good practice. The conference, Developing Communities for Health – held for two days at the University of Salford in Greater Manchester from 7 September 1999 – was the result.

This conference, attended by some 120 delegates, was energised and stimulating. Keynote speakers from the United Kingdom and North America provided a framework and back-cloth against which much experience was shared, insights received and a momentum was generated which should help to realise Sir Kenneth's aspirations.

This book is intended to enable the key points to reach a wider audience in the North West and beyond – an audience which must be reached if community development is to come of age and permeate, in a strategic way, all areas of everyday life, and public services which impact on health.

Since the conference there has been a change of Minister for Public Health, with Tessa Jowell handing the baton on to Yvette Cooper. Some three years into this government's administration, the incorporation of the 1999 Duncan Lecture into this conference report seems a valuable way of publishing the new Minister's speech and taking stock of the policies for public health which have so far been put in place, and against which Communities Developing for Health must now be tested.

Professor John Ashton CBE
Regional director of public health/Regional medical officer,
NHS Executive North West

August 2000

Community development and the Government's policy agenda

Tessa Jowell MP
Minister for public health

I would like to outline and clarify the Government's approach to community development in public health, and to indicate some areas for reflection that you may wish to consider during your discussions.

Community development is central to the new public health and it should be a core part of a modernised healthcare system, and integral to policy development across all those issues that influence the community's health. Community development can be a complex and contentious area of public policy, and an industry has grown up in recent years seeking definitions of what it is and what it is not. Let us focus instead on areas of agreement and look at the increasing evidence now becoming available, of the ethical and effective community development interventions that work for the improvement of health in its widest sense.

There are at least five types of community development activity that may improve the health of the population and which might inform the evolving public health strategy.

1. Community development involves institutional and capacity building. Government cannot effectively promote the development of active and empowered communities without also fostering the corresponding organisational development in the institutions that will need to respond to them. In this sense community development activity should be aimed at developing the framework of organisational capacity, procedures, rights and structures, through which citizens and communities can effect social change for themselves.

2. Community development involves fostering the growth of the voluntary or third sector, and this involves offering training, resources and other support for non-governmental groups and social welfare societies working for and within communities to improve the

quality of life of their most vulnerable members. In the UK many such groups date back to Victorian times, and many have specific public health objectives, making them invaluable partners in health promotion more generally.

3. Community development can be understood as social action: this involves communities of people taking action for civil and human rights. Sometimes such groups may work in conflict with the state, commercial interests or global economic systems, and this can be uncomfortable for all concerned. But by and large this is the sign of a healthy democracy, and in recent times such activities have been particularly prominent in influencing social change for health and environmental improvement at local and national levels.

4. Community development can be seen as the development of safe and healthy neighbourhood settings. The development of supportive environments for health has a central role in government strategy for broader health improvement: it involves the community itself in taking action on health needs in specific settings, such as health-promoting schools, workplaces, and neighbourhoods. Such action requires mediation and support from a wide range of other partners and stakeholders, and evidence shows that such community partnerships have a real potential to reduce crime, increase safety and promote a wide range of mental and social health improvements.

5. Particularly from an international perspective, community development is most often understood as popular community education. Specific techniques developed in South America are now widely adopted in other parts of the world; these focus on raising awareness, skills and competencies of individuals and communities, thereby empowering them to take action to change the environments which determine the chances in their lives. Such community education initiatives underpin a number of public health education strategies identified in Saving Lives, our White Paper published last July.

All of these perspectives and ways of seeing community development activity have a great deal to offer the development of public health capacity and action, and they should be given support both by public and private sector agencies.

Although community development can be an effective strategy for achieving a wide range of social objectives, I want to concentrate specifically on its contribution to public health. Throughout the world, healthcare systems are being reviewed and refocused. Most reviews have concluded that healthcare systems have understandably focused their resources on treating the proportion of the population who are ill at any one time, and the NHS is no exception to this. One unintended consequence has been that investment in interventions for those who certainly will be ill if preventive action is not taken has been neglected; coupled with this has been an increasing realisation that health is mostly created or destroyed where people work, live and play — long before they access the healthcare system. It follows that if we want to achieve real health improvements for the whole population, and particularly for those with the worst health, then we need to address the causes of health, not just the consequences of disease. These can only be effectively addressed outside the formal healthcare system, in partnership with the community in the context of their everyday lives, and for this task community development is a key strategy.

Population health research since the early 1990s, particularly in countries in transition in Central and Eastern Europe (where for instance the average life expectancy for Russian men has fallen recently below the official retirement age), suggests that rapid social change and decreases in social capital, and the erosion of civic society and poor institutional performance, have major consequences for population health. The solutions to these problems lie in rebuilding social capital, civic society, trust, participation, social inclusion and community-based support through strategies which are part of community development.

Community development has the potential to promote efficiency in healthcare provision, equity in health, and increased community access to health-promoting resources. There is, for instance, a pressing need to identify and improve the health outcomes – as well as the disease treatment outcomes – of healthcare investment and activity in hospitals. This drives the need to connect healthcare services to supportive community infrastructures capable of assisting rehabilitation, social support and the promotion of independence. These will not develop without planned and well supported community development interventions.

Looking to the future, we can see that demands on the health and social welfare services will grow dramatically in the new millennium. According to the World Health Organisation, key issues for the future include:
- the changing role of women, brought about by their rising life expectancy and a falling birth-rate
- a decreasing involvement by men in paid employment, brought about by earlier retirement
- increasing length of adolescence, brought about by increased time in education and the growing gap between biological and social or emotional adulthood
- an increase in the elderly population, particularly in women
- the increased consequences of relationship stress and family breakdown
- the increase in the incidence of lone parenthood
- an increase in dispersed nuclear families missing out on social and family support

- the polarisation of work-rich and work-poor families
- a reduction in social cohesion
- increasingly insecure tenure of employment for those who work, coupled with greater demands for geographical mobility
- an increased level of disease and illness related to environmental degradation, damage and pollution.

Doctors and healthcare workers are increasingly dealing with the consequences of these larger 'macro' social and economic issues for their patients. Indeed such factors are apparent in increased referral for a wide range of clinical services throughout the healthcare system. But there is a growing understanding that these problems cannot be effectively dealt with or left in the consultation room. Such problems lie beyond the sovereignty of any one individual and are only capable of resolution by the development of partnership between government and communities.

So what has the Government done to enable community development? A very wide range of government policy has now been enacted that specifically has community development and partnership at the centre of its strategies for action. This is an important part of the Government's commitment to cross-departmental policy-making for public health. For example, the Department of Environment, Transport and the Regions has published policies supportive of community development, including modernising local government (In Touch With the People), guidance on enhancing public participation in local government, and Local Agenda 21. Resources for community development action have also been made available through social regeneration budgets. Many new government policy initiatives, such as the Sure Start programme and the Crime & Disorder Act specifically require cross-departmental action and the collaboration of community organisations, and through the Social Exclusion Unit key policies such as neighbourhood renewal and a wide range of other strategies specifically require or support community development.

Specific policy initiatives, such as Building The Future Together, reflect the Government's wish to help rebuild a sense of community in the United Kingdom, and have been specifically designed to assist better partnership with the voluntary sector, and also to promote volunteering. Enabling legislation has allowed Lottery and Millennium Fund moneys to be provided for Healthy Living Centres and other health promotion initiatives that will have a clear focus on community-based prevention and empowerment for health improvement.

Within the Department of Health itself a range of new systems, structures and resources will allow community development to be integrated into mainstream healthcare activity. Central to these are Health Improvement Programmes, Health Action Zones and the forthcoming restructuring and new resources available for public health development. But there is a limit to what can be achieved from the top down, even with the enabling frameworks already established. Much of the community development action that will make a real difference to the quality of people's lives must be developed locally, and such initiatives might include:

- the development of linked and integrated multi-agency community development plans, bringing together the key players for community development
- professional and organisational development and training for community development in health
- the development of health-promoting settings within neighbourhoods
- the routine integration of community development values and processes within the mainstream activity of the NHS, particularly within the context of primary care.

So in conclusion, let me reiterate the key importance that the development of community development empowerment strategies has in meeting our very clear aims for tackling the root causes of ill health, reducing the unjustifiable toll of preventable death and improving the health of the worst-off. And we are now at a position where we can move on from defining the problems and dedicate more time and resources to solutions, to action, and the delivery of change. I see community development as being central to this task and I look forward to reviewing the outcomes of the discussions in Salford as a way of taking us closer to those goals that we both share.

Building community capacity from the bottom up

Dr John Kretzmann
Co-Director, Asset Based Community Development Institute
Institute for Policy Research, Northwestern University, USA

I am not a health professional. My last 35 years have been mostly centred in communities. I came up in the civil rights movement in the United States and early on learnt that some of my best teachers were not people in universities but people who lived in dirt-floored shacks in the American South.

I want to reflect on how we have been learning from communities, mostly in North America, about this question: How does the practice and understanding of community health bring together the two worlds of communities and health professionals, who need to be partners in this work?

Let me start with a brief set of observations on why somebody out of a community development background should be part of a health discussion. This question came up for us in Chicago about three years ago and we prevailed on some of our friends in the medical school at Northwestern University to help us think about the relationship between health and community. We asked them the epidemiological question, where does health come from?

They said that if we wanted to boil down the millions of pages written about this, these five things would determine whether or not people are healthy:
1. People's personal behaviour. Do we eat well? Do we exercise? Are we stopping smoking?
2. Our social relations. Are we part of a network, extended kin, community – for both mental and physical health. Are there supportive sets of relationships in our lives?
3. The state of our physical environment. Can we breathe the air? Drink the water? Is the food safe to eat?
4. Our economic status. When we need to enter the marketplace, can we do so in a powerful enough way to get what we need?

5. Access to therapy. When we are sick do we have access to doctors and nurses, clinics and hospitals and so on?

(Some people say there might also be a spiritual dimension to health.)

We then asked two more questions of our colleagues in medical school. First, is there any agreement in the literature about which is the most important determinant of health? They laughed at us. They said there is no agreement. We asked a second question: Can we go at it the other way – is there any agreement in the literature about which is the least important determinant of health? They stopped laughing and said that everybody knows what is the least important: access to therapy. About 10 per cent of the contribution to whether or not a person is healthy through life has to do with whether or not that person, when sick, has access to therapy. In the production of health the other four factors, in some order or other, are all more important than whether or not there is access to therapy.

In the United States this means that we spend about 95 per cent of our policy deliberations, and about that proportion of our dollars, focused on the least important determinant of health. Obviously it is critically important for people when they are sick to have access to the kind of professional help and healing that we all want. But that is a discussion about healing sick people, it is not a discussion about the production of health.

So the last place we might go to produce health or to strategise about producing health would be a hospital. In fact we would be driven into the community for a discussion around changing personal behaviour - most often affected by peers - strengthening social relationships, making the physical environment safer and more healthy and bringing advances in economic status. So that is my rationale for being part of this discussion.

How do we think about the community not simply as consumers of therapy, but as producers of health? It is the production factor. How does the community produce health? It has become clear in our research over the last ten years in the US that the community is a producer of outcomes that we all wish for, not only in the health field, but in other areas as well, for example, the feeling of safety and well-being.

We know increasingly that communities are the producers of well-being for young people, for the elderly, for the family, and that the social networks and the social capital available in the community are the primary ingredients for the production of about 65 per cent of the jobs that are being produced in the US economy. This focus on the community as producer has led us to ask the question: Why are communities not doing more of it? What stands in the way of communities producing such outcomes?

There is one particular massive road block, at least in North America, which was suggested to us during four years of visiting many of the lowest income communities in the United States. We put a question to leaders in those communities that they had not been asked very often before: we asked them about what was working in their communities, what was succeeding, what was giving them hope. We gathered the top 200 success stories they gave us into a book, Building Communities from the Inside Out, thinking about the lessons that we could begin to learn if we were attentive to success at the local level, rather than failure.

For us the major lesson came from a great teacher of mine, Mrs Edna Johnson, a black woman who had lived her entire life in the South Bronx in New York City. In the US the South Bronx was for a couple of decades the absolute symbol of urban decay. But if something was working – young people creating new enterprises, a health clinic being brought into the community and staffed by local folks, a school being made better, a park being brought back to life – and if we were to scratch the surface a little bit we would find that Mrs Johnson was involved. She would be putting people together, creating networks and connections, prodding the activity. She was just a genius at community building.

I asked Mrs Johnson how the South Bronx became the symbol of urban decay. She paused for a moment and I could see her scrolling through potential answers, all of which would have been true, about the lack of investment, about crumbling institutions, about lack of public sector and government involvement, the power of racism. But what she finally said to me was this, 'The worst thing that ever happened to us in my community was that we got put into a prison. I am talking about a prison made up of other people's ideas about who we are in my community.'

She said, 'I go down to City Hall and talk to public officials, or I go and make a speech in the suburbs, I introduce myself and I say I am Mrs Johnson, and somebody always asks where I am from, and I say I am from the South Bronx. And the minute I say the words "South Bronx", I can see what happens. Into their heads flow an immense number of images and ideas about my community. And what is so powerful about those ideas is that they are all about what we do not have, our needs and our problems and our deficiencies. That is what I mean by a prison.'

My friend Mrs Johnson was reminding us that no community on the face of the earth has ever been built except by the skills, knowledge and contributions of the people who live there – not on their needs, deficiencies and emptinesses. And she was also reminding us that we have spent the last four or five decades building huge institutions and systems whose major message to Mrs Johnson and her neighbours, and other low-income communities across the United States, is: We know what is important about you and your community, it is your emptiness, your needs, your problems and your deficiencies. If you want to get plugged into government resources, university interests, media coverage or private foundation funding, you should get better at telling us about your needs and problems and deficiencies, and we will reward you with money from the outside, or with experts who know better. We will teach you how to do things like needs surveys and make sure that they are the first way you communicate your reality to the outside world. This is the prison dance.

The consequences of that in the United States have been devastating. The worst consequence is when a person in a community who has been told this over and over again begins to think that it is true, and begins to say, 'Well that must be who I am, I cannot possibly raise my children, I need somebody who is better at it than I am, knows more, has more credentials. I cannot possibly attend to the health of my family, or my block, or my neighbourhood, I need somebody else to do that for me. I cannot possibly make my community safe, I need the police to come in and do that for me.' And so we have created a structure in which people hand their power off quite willingly and lose their capacity to act, to create health, and to produce safety and well-being for themselves and their families.

The other thing it does is to create a consensus of hopelessness. My 16-year-old neighbour told me earlier this summer that he was not going back to school because he could not see a future for himself in his neighbourhood, and he was not about to invest in his future as an individual when his context could not promise him a future. And if I am Bill Clinton in the White House and I keep getting funding requests from neighbourhoods and cities across the United States, I say, 'They are asking me to pour money down an ever-deepening hole,' because the game is, if you want more money next year you go back and say, 'I am sorry, we did everything we could but we failed. We have more pregnant teens this year than we did last year, so give us more dollars.' It is a game that rewards failure, and therefore creates hopelessness from the bottom of society to the top, from the inside of the community to the outside.

The wonderful news is that there are thousands and thousands of people across the US and across the UK who have said with Mrs Johnson, 'That is somebody else's idea about who we are, and what we really need to do is to create our own idea of who we are. And the starting point is to map, if you will, our communities' fullness, which we will call assets.' What do we have in our community? If we are to be strategic and powerful about attacking the empty part of the glass, the place to start is the full part of the glass. And so we are seeing, in community after community, people unlearning the prison dance and re-learning a discipline which asks, 'What are the major categories of giftedness or resourcefulness – power, if you will – that we have in our local community?'

I would suggest that three categories of assets define every community:

1. Every community has people who live there with their 'skilledness', their resourcefulness, their knowledge, their giftedness.
2. Every community has some secondary array of small, voluntary, face-to-face associations, the choirs, softball teams, cricket clubs, churches, block clubs and the various manifestations of local connectedness around voluntary efforts.
3. Every community has some combination of local institutions, public, private, non-profit. (An institution is a place where people are paid to do the work, an association is a place where the members do the work.)

So thinking about the production of health changes when people begin to refocus on assets rather than on needs. Let me give a couple of illustrations. There is a 'core' at the level of the individual resident which can be uncovered with a little bit of proactive work by community builders, community development and community health people. People have begun using a tool called a capacity inventory, or strengths inventory or skills interview, a way of uncovering the giftedness of people.

A couple of years ago a community group in a very poor community in Chicago became terrifically concerned about the infant mortality rate in their neighbourhood, after seeing it rise to about 35 per 1000. They decided that whoever was in charge of doing something about infant mortality in their community was not doing a terrific job, and they could invent other ways of doing it that might work better. They did the politics and persuaded the state government to give them a 'waiver'. They diverted 95 per cent of the money spent for infant mortality work in their neighbourhood to this community organisation, which was housed in a church. They found 15 young mothers who were raising healthy children, sometimes up to five kids under the age of eight, and began convening these 15 moms around the question of how did they bear healthy children, and how were they raising healthy children. What were their secrets? What did they know about nutrition and exercise? Did they know about regular care?

They gave them some basic prenatal training and some additional nutritional training, and said to the 15 moms, would you mind beginning to visit your neighbours? Take about five a week. Just drop in and talk to other moms on your block. And they began doing that. And they found it was great fun, to meet their neighbours and to talk about common issues in motherhood and so on. It became a real movement in that neighbourhood, women talking to each other about how to raise healthy children, how to have a healthy pregnancy. Within three years that approach of using healthy moms in the community meant that the infant mortality rate was reduced from 33-34 per 1000 to 17 per 1000, and they are still working on it. They cut it in half simply by asking how they could use local folks, local resources to do that work.

Similarly a group called the West Side Health Authority in a very low-income community in Chicago has begun redefining the production of health as their own work in the neighbourhood. When the last clinic closed in this neighbourhood, they organised and met frequently for six months and decided on a two-pronged attack: they would do everything they could to mobilise the community to get a health centre back. After three years they were successful, the clinic re-opened, they got some public dollars committed to it and they had a large celebration.

The second path they took was to say that even when they had had the clinic before they had not been all that healthy, so something else must be needed to produce health in this community. And they began thinking about a block-by-block approach. They hired five health organisers, attached each one to a local church, and began going block by block, to find the three healthiest people on each block. Then they began convening the healthy people to talk to each other about their secrets of health, exercise, diet, grandma's remedies, whatever they were using. Then they began saying to the healthy people, in the same way the other group had said to the moms, could you start visiting everybody else on this block? Could you start seeing if there are some of the practices that you engage in, particularly the ones that you enjoy most, that you would like to share with your neighbours? That movement has been going on in that neighbourhood for about two-and-a-half years now, and the visits to emergency rooms and to clinics have been cut about in half. So it looks like the people are staying much healthier.

We have begun to think that there is a two-part pledge at the centre of every committed healthy community builder. The first part of the pledge is that everybody in a community is gifted, everybody has some fullness; even gang members or people who are coming out of prison. It is a critical first step, because it means that we need to change some language. We have all kinds of language that label people as ungifted and unfull. The language of welfare is like that. 'Recipient' – an empty person who gets stuff from the outside; 'client' – an empty person, and 'patient' – somebody who is pretty powerless. We have to look instead for language about neighbours, partners and friends, that has fullness about it.

The second part of the pledge, at least in a North American context, is equally difficult. If we say on the one hand that everybody has gifts, strengths and resources, the measure of a healthy community in one sense is: How many people are giving their gifts? So the second part of the pledge is that everybody contributes. The way we all belong to communities is by contributing; the way we get marginalised is by people looking at us as if we have nothing to contribute and therefore never asking. That is the experience of welfare in many of our communities, those who are too poor cannot contribute. It is the experience of being young:, 'You are too young, you cannot contribute. You are at most the leader of tomorrow.' It is the experience of many elders, 'You are too old, we will not ask you to contribute any more.' It is the experience of many people with mental and physical disabilities and challenges, 'You are on the sidelines, we will never ask you to contribute.'

So we have been particularly interested in the ways that communities have been mobilising to ask people on their margins what do you have, what do you know, and how would you like to contribute what you have and what you know?

Let me give one example about the power that this can represent. The folks in a group of mostly black Baptist churches in Cincinnati, Ohio had been trying to make their community more healthy by feeding people in a soup kitchen, and they fed about 300 people a night. After doing that for many years, they gradually became dissatisfied. They began saying, 'Could we do something more than feeding people? Could we connect them more fully to the centre of community and economy, and really work on their health with them?' They decided that they were not doing that because they did not know the people they were feeding. Then they thought, 'But wait a minute, we do know something about them, we know about their emptiness, that many of them are fighting drug and alcohol abuse, that many of them do not have a job or a home. We know about their emptiness, we do not know about their fullness.' And so they did a survey, asking close to 500 people about their gifts, skills and dreams.

The survey form says, 'Thanks for coming over. Did anybody talk to you about what this gift exchange is all about, what you understand it to be?' At the start of every interview, they gave a brightly coloured little box with a ribbon, made by the young people, to the person to be interviewed. Inside is a key chain, and on the chain is an inscription, 'Your gift is your key to your community.' Then they ask about gifts, the abilities they were born with. 'What positive qualities do people say you have?' 'Who are the people in your life that you give to? How do you do that? What do you give that makes you feel good about giving?' Under skills, 'What do you enjoy doing? If you could start a business, what would it be? What do you like to do that people would pay you to do?' (all the research around entrepreneurship says that that is the critical question). And then dreams, 'What are they? If you could snap your fingers and be doing anything, what would it be?'

These are not open-toe sandal questions. The walls of the soup kitchen are now covered with brightly calligraphed photographs and drawings of hundreds of people, and a list of their gifts, skills and dreams. The dreams and skills and gifts are being changed and connected all the time. The second thing one sees is the result of the answer to a question about skills. More than half the people who came to the soup kitchen, when asked, 'What do you like to do best? What do you really do well?' said, 'I love to cook.' After a while the church folks began to understand what they were hearing – not just about a skill, cooking. People were telling them, 'I do not want to be on this side of the table any more, with you over on the other side of the table cooking for me, and serving me. Because as long as you are on the other side of the table and I am over here, you are a human being and I am not, you belong to this community, and are valued, and I am not. I want to come around to the other side of the table and I want to cook with you. And I want to be part of the servers here.'

Within a matter of months the church folk had re-done the rules of the soup kitchen so that those who volunteered there cooked and served and ate. And for those who came in off the street for a meal, it is the same. I could not tell who were the volunteers and who were the people off the streets, because everybody was doing everything. They had found a way, in other words, to at least reduce, if not eliminate, the natural power differentiation between the server and the served, the helper and the helped, the doctor and the patient, and they had begun to re-create a setting in which power was more or less shared more or less equally, in more or less a partnership.

This is where the open-toe sandal feel-good stuff begins to translate into hard outcomes. Once the church people started relating in this new way, they began to discover the skills of the folks in the soup kitchen, and found teachers, carpenters, plumbers and artists, and began plugging them into the world of work, back into the middle of community as well. They found people who loved to sing, and put them in choirs; people who loved to produce art, and put them in charge of the walls, and then a whole community mural movement took off in that neighbourhood. They found ways for at least a good portion of those hundreds of clients in the soup kitchen to rediscover their power as co-producers of community and economy in that setting.

The lesson for me was that if they could do that with folks in off the street, many down and out for some period of time, why can we not do it for everybody else on the margins of our communities, folks who are too poor, too young, too old, too disabled, too whatever, to be part of the healthy community movement? So what we have seen over and over again is the power of changing the focus, never losing sight of the fact that there is emptiness in every individual community and nation, but always rediscovering that the first set of powers to be mobilised have to do with people who are no longer recipients and no longer clients but are now really powerful. The word we have learnt to use in the United States, and some of you in the UK, is 'citizens'. They are citizens in the sense that they have the idea that they can act effectively in public, that the community is their business, the block is their business, and the health of the neighbourhood is their business. So the production of health in a local setting is also, it seems to us, the production of democracy.

As we go into the 21st century this will be one of the critical challenges. In South Africa I saw a community that understood this so deeply that their health agenda was first of all about getting choir uniforms, and secondly about getting soccer shoes. They understood health as a product of community activities that had everybody involved. It is a struggle, though, because we have too much of the old way of thinking still hanging on.

The last thing I would say about this approach is that we have in a 'healthy communities' movement the opportunity to spread some hope, to allow people to see the possibility that something effective can be done. And that is really exciting.

An historical perspective on community development in the UK – power, politics and radical action

Paul Henderson
Director of practice development, Community Development Foundation

It is difficult to talk about the history of community development, as opposed to hearing a local person talk about the things they are involved in, or hearing practitioners talk about their work, without it losing its edge. And that is a key point: community development has to have an edge to it.

I do not intend to go through the chronology of community development from Year Dot to the end of the Nineties. Instead, I will take a thematic approach, introducing historical perspectives within six themes:

1. The changing auspices of community development
2. The tension between generalist profession/intervention or an approach taken into specialisms
3. The relationship between the voluntary and statutory sectors in community development
4. The importance of internationalism
5. Social movement or profession?
6. Conservatism and radicalism.

I would argue that each of these six is crucial to an understanding of the history of community development.

1. The changing auspices of community development

With one or two rare exceptions, community development has not existed in its own right. It has always needed a backer, a sponsor, which could take it along. Pre-1960s, the education profession played a key role by introducing community development through community associations, youth work and adult education. At the end of the

1960s, there was a tussle between the education profession and the social work profession over who would be the sponsor of community development, as it began to receive recognition in the UK, through a number of important committees and reports such as the Seebohm Report in 1968.[1] Most people would agree that social work won that tussle and took community development forward into the Seventies. (A different discussion concerns how social work handled that responsibility and drew upon community development to develop what it called community social work, or patch social work.)

As we ended the Seventies and went into the Eighties, social work began to lose interest in community development, for all sorts of reasons. Community development then came under the auspices of economic development, and more latterly regeneration in the Nineties. So it left behind its two original sponsors, education and social work, and became closely aligned with what is now a very powerful movement for community economic development and regeneration.

There are important provisos to make. In Scotland, for instance, community education is still important to community development, because Scotland has a much stronger community education sector than England.

Is any of this surprising? Surely community development has just followed the money and has been resource-led. Clearly it is no accident that community development now finds most of its work where the funding lies, in regeneration. But it is more profound than that. If we look at the history of community development in more detail we can see how it has become more relevant to different interests at particular times. One example is the differing interest of trusts and foundations in supporting community development: in the late 1960s and throughout the 1970s the Gulbenkian Foundation was a very important strategic funder, albeit on a small scale compared to statutory funding. Arguably the Joseph Rowntree Foundation has taken over that role from the Gulbenkian in the 1990s. Community development seems to have a fascination for different professions and interest groups at certain times, and so they have sought to harness it to their cause.

One effect of this constant changing of the auspices under which community development has functioned has been a very weak infrastructure of training institutions, training courses (especially in higher education), membership organisations and support bodies, of which my organisation is an example. They are all poorly funded, often struggling to be refunded year to year. So at the time that many organisations and interests are picking up on community development or looking at it again, they are dealing with something which has a very weak infrastructure.

2. Generalist-specialist tensions

The generalist position argues that there is a core or 'spine' of community development which has its own values, knowledge base and set of skills, which need to be constantly argued for, updated and disseminated. In this thinking, generalists therefore need to permeate other organisations such as the health service and local authorities with those core ideas. The history of community development shows that this has always been the intention, in the way it has been picked up by specialist organisations or professions such as social work, health and economic development, who have sought to mould it to meet their own interests. This is quite justifiable, but it has led to people wondering what community development is, because often someone in the health service, social work or education will therefore only understand community development from their own perspective.

Settings where community development has been seen as a core, a generalist interventional profession include the United Nations, which has always had a strong interest in community development, both as the League of Nations before the Second World War and as the UN immediately after it, issuing some important documents and policy statements. At the end of the nineteenth century, there was the Settlement Movement and the establishment of settlements, mainly in London, and the Church Organisation Society (this surreptitiously makes the point that the history of community development did not start in 1968). There was also a strong community development element in helping people settle into the post-1945 new towns and new estates.

The Gulbenkian Report of 1968[2] is usually seen as the starting gun for community development in the UK. This important report argued very strongly for community development to exist in its own right as a core activity. The Community Development Projects also started in 1968, and ran through to about 1976. These were 12 projects funded by central government in association with local authorities, working closely with universities, and are very important in the history of community development. The mass of documentation about them is still used on the few training courses there are, partly because they were an important example of using community development as a central, core activity. A final example is the Standing Conference for Community Development (SCCD), the umbrella organisation for community development in the UK.

In contrast, specialisms or professions which have taken on community development as part of their own activity include the youth service in the 1970s, community social work in the 1970s and the early 1980s, and probation work. They all had a strong interest in community work and imported many of its ideas and methods, and set up a large number of experiments. In the Eighties there were community health projects and economic development, and Local Agenda 21 in the Nineties.

One of the effects of this tension between generalism and specialism has been that practitioners do not quite know how to handle certain situations, probably because they are not sure whether to be drawn into their own profession or occupation, or to stay within the sphere of community development. Brian Munday of the University of Kent says 'a constant tension for community work has been a need to look inwards, to the building up of the knowledge and skills base of a discipline, as well as looking outwards to influence other disciplines'.

Community development has not made the running in all these examples. The receptivity of the different professions and organisations to the ideas of community development has also been significant. Social work was receptive to community development in the Seventies, while the health sector was arguably less so. But now the health service is very receptive to notions of community development, while social work shows no interest whatsoever, as far as I can see.

3. The voluntary/statutory relationship

This too has a tension built into it, probably a very positive tension. On the whole, initiatives in the history of community development have occurred in the voluntary sector. In the early and mid-Sixties some very important community development initiatives took place entirely within the voluntary sector, for example, the North Kensington Community Project, or the Nottingdale Project. Key players from that project went on to influence the committees referred to earlier, such as the Seebohm Committee and the Gulbenkian Committee, which resulted in the Gulbenkian Report. It was not until the early Seventies, when people like myself were taken on as community development workers within social services departments, that the statutory sector began to engage with community development.

We see that pattern being repeated throughout the history of community development: initiatives beginning in a voluntary setting, then trying to move into the statutory setting. One important aspect of that is the history of significant individuals in community development – all of them have done their work within the voluntary community sector. Len White was very important in the community associations and new town work in the late Forties and early Fifties; Ann Power, who is now a professor at the London School of Economics, started her professional life as a community worker in a voluntary church project in Islington in the late Sixties and early Seventies, and went on to play an important policy role in making connections between radical community action in the voluntary sector and the need for housing departments and housing professionals to incorporate community development in their work.

There is an energy in the voluntary sector which is not always found in the statutory sector. Churches and voluntary organisations such as the Church Urban Fund, the Children's Society, Save the Children and the Alinsky-based organisation Broad-Based Organising often work in ways only found in the voluntary sector. And in rural areas of the UK (largely neglected by community development in favour of urban areas until the Nineties) very small, poorly funded community councils are now asking their local authorities to show an interest in community development.

There is also the matter of the project culture in the UK. We love the project culture – apparently. We love to set up projects for three to five years in the hope that they will then be taken on by some other body, usually someone in the statutory sector. Organisations like my own have been as guilty of this as any – we set up projects, usually funded for two years, always in partnership with other organisations, in the hope that they will be taken into the mainstream work of the local authority or health organisation. History will tell us that this happens rather rarely. The transfer across from the voluntary to the statutory relies mainly upon particular individuals, upon work being written up or presented at conferences in certain ways, upon people almost campaigning.

4. Internationalism

My brief was to look at community development in the UK, but it is difficult to do that in isolation from international developments.

First, there were the people who came back to the UK after working in community development in the Colonial Service (a piece of embarrassing history!). When the ex-colonies became independent nations people like Batten came back and were very instrumental in starting community development in the UK. In a similar way, people who have worked for development agencies such as Oxfam have come back and engaged in community action in the UK, as volunteers or staff. People from other countries have also visited the UK and become involved – for example the Canadian, Ilys Booker, brought ideas from Sicily, where she had worked with Danello Dolci, and from Canada, when she came to work with the Nottingdale Project in the 1960s. Harry Specht, a US social work professor who visited the UK regularly in the late Sixties and into the Seventies, is another example.

The importance of ideas should not be underestimated. The ideas of Paulo Freire about conscientisation and education as a key part of community development are arguably now embedded in our understanding of community development. They have been most important in terms of sustaining the theory and values of community development in the UK.[3]

There have been other examples closer to home. We invited Dutch practitioners to visit the UK and talk about they way they had developed regional centres to support community development, and we translated much of their material.

Equally important is the networking between people in different countries, local people and practitioners, and collaboration between different countries. There are now European and international organisations that can help those processes. Finally, the policies of international organisations are also influential, such as the World Health Organisation's Health for All initiative, which is crucial for many of those working in the health service; another example is the UN Convention on the Rights of the Child, which has played a key role in work on children's participation.

5. Social movement or profession?

This is an old chestnut, but an important chestnut. Is community development a social movement, or a profession? It is probably a bit of both. A very sharp debate took place in the 1970s, and I am not proposing to go over it again, but it is important to recognise that the debate took place. There are two points to note.

The first is to emphasise that it was a genuine debate because it forced us to define community development, and to look at the evidence for community development happening independently of professional support.

There are many examples up and down the country of small-scale projects which do not depend on professional input, and which explain the use of words like 'self-help' and 'self-reliance', referring to those small-scale initiatives that people do on their own. Those initiatives – that community development – will go on, even if every professional in community development walked out.

Alongside those initiatives there have been much higher profile social movements, such as the squatters' movements (immediately post-war and in the Sixties), protests against new roads, against environmental dereliction or hazards. These all meet the criteria of Piven and Cloward, who studied the 1970s protest movements in the United States. They said that the defining characteristics must be a change in consciousness, when people realise they can challenge the system themselves, and a change in behaviour, leading to effective collective action.

The debate – social movement or profession? – is a slightly spurious one, because both need each other, and it is not a very meaningful distinction unless defined more closely. What is important to emphasise is that professional community development needs social movements, they are the lifeblood, the energy that is required for professional community development to mean anything. And vice versa, at some point social movements need professional community development when, historically, they become organisations, either formally or informally.

The second key point under this theme is the sea change that came from a critique of community development, which said that community development had become trapped in the neighbourhood, both literally and metaphorically. It talked about working with local people, mobilising them, but critics started asking: What difference has it made? How has it changed communities? We listened to those criticisms and took them seriously. In response, from about 1980 up to the present day, in addition to work at the neighbourhood level, community development has also been done at the organisational level and at the policy level, by those who are serious about introducing change and helping communities.

This has not been an easy change, but some might say it is a sign that community development has grown up. Organisations have taken community development on board as a central part of their own strategies, for example local authorities such as Haringey in the 1970s and 1980s, Strathclyde in the 1970s, when community development was the lynchpin of its whole social strategy, Sheffield until recently, Kirklees, Liverpool and some NHS trusts. The major report put out in 1993 by the Association of Metropolitan Authorities, Local Authorities and Community Development – a major report sponsored by local authorities coming out in favour of community development – symbolises that change.

6. Conservatism versus radicalism

One reason for the debate between conservatism and radicalism is the notion of community development as a broad church, which makes it very vulnerable to misuse, for example the way the United States used community development in some of its overseas programmes. In the UK some would argue that community development has been used as a conservative mechanism, particularly in post-riot situations or where every other attempt has been made to do something about a particular community or estate and they have all failed, 'so let us put in three community development workers and see what they can do'.

There has also been a debate between different ideological positions, between a radical or socialist perspective (the Community Development Project mentioned earlier was part of that stream) on the one hand, and the more pluralist or liberal position on the other. It is a less important debate these days than it was in the Seventies or Eighties, it has to be said.

The most important aspect of the discussion about conservatism and radicalism is the way that community development has sought to relate to other movements or issues in its history. The feminist critique of community development, as not being aware of what was happening in communities, was a very powerful critique in the Seventies and Eighties, and particularly poignant given that most community organising in neighbourhoods is done by women.

The critique from a black perspective was even more hard-hitting. There is still an enormous gulf in the UK between white-based community development and black-based community development, with bridges built between the two very occasionally. Black communities feel that community development has not been particularly helpful to them, and in a sense they have gone their own way, engaging with racism and raising the issue of ethnicity, leaving community development to one side. The disability movement and the users' movement have also given lessons to community development about participation and involvement.

THE IMPORTANCE OF THE HISTORICAL PERSPECTIVE

The historical perspective is important because it helps us in the UK to locate ourselves in terms of the rise and fall and rise again of community development in different settings. This applies particularly to health.

Second, it is important to track the changes in community development and the way it has been taken up by different professions and the way it has sought to engage with policy makers. Community development has sought to rebut the criticism that it is only about doing things in neighbourhoods — lots of activity but not much strategy — and it has begun to be quite effective in doing so. History helps us understand that.

Third, history helps to relate community development to other themes and to the wider context. Much of what happened to community development was the product of any one time, such as the Thatcher years and now the Blair years.

Fourth, with apologies to EH Carr, it helps us to learn lessons. We can see where mistakes were made and where community development has been effective.

Finally, history shows the real challenge that community development poses us. It is not an easy option, many things can go wrong, from the best of intentions, particularly when we place community development within the context of anti-poverty and social inclusion work.

Why is this perspective particularly important for the health service? First, it is important for health to understand the extent to which communities already have experiences of community activity and community organising. Some of those experiences are very positive, some of them are quite negative. I have recently finished a piece of work in Merseyside where in at least two of the neighbourhoods it proved difficult to start any new initiative because local people were feeling so embittered and angry from their previous experiences of external agencies that it was not right to try to introduce another one.

Second, health has to learn from history how to relate to the broader picture. Community development is holistic, broad-based, generalist, which has practical implications as well as ideas implications. It means that often it will be important to work with local people on issues that do not appear to have much to do with health, if one is to help mobilise them.

Finally, it is important in the health context to go for the long haul. Short-term projects do little to strengthen communities. We are dealing with long-term processes of change. That is why that terrible phrase, 'turning around particularly troubled council estates', gets in the way of one's thinking about community development, because that is not what community development is about. It is about contributing to the development of those communities, not about 'turning them around' in some quick whizz-kid way. Go for the long haul.

Bibliography

1. HMSO (1968), Report of the Committee on Local Authority and Allied Personal Social Services ('Seebohm Report'), Cmnd3702

2. Calouste Gulbenkian Roundation (1968), Community Work and Social Change: A Report on Training, London, Longman

3. Freire P (1972), Pedagogy of the Oppressed, Penguin; Freire P (1974), Education: The Practice of Freedom Writers and Readers Publishing Corporation; Freire P (1985), The Politics of Education: Culture, Power and Liberation, Macmillan

Organisational development and professional change as a prerequisite for equality and partnership with local people

Community development and primary care groups – accountability and equity in action?

Philip Crowley
Newcastle Community Development in Health, Newcastle upon Tyne

INTRODUCTION

This article sets out to share some ideas about the value for Primary Care Groups (PCGs) of engaging with local communities in a developmental way. Most of the ideas arise from the experience of a community development project linked to primary care in the West End of Newcastle since 1995.

Obviously many recent policy initiatives have highlighted the need for greater public accountability and participation for communities in decision-making, such as The New NHS – Modern and Dependable; Saving Lives (the White Paper on public health), Health Action Zones and Modernising Local Government.

What are the advantages of involving the public? I would suggest that the following are some good reasons to develop a positive relationship with the local communities:
- It leads to a greater understanding of local health issues and new approaches to tackling problems that may be more effective – it challenges traditional ways of doing things.
- Dialogue improves relationships and mutual understanding.
- The public may be your greatest ally.
- It helps the health system to better understand the connection between social issues such as racial harassment and health.
- There is a policy requirement to achieve this.
- It is healthy for local people to achieve more control through participation.
- It is the community's right and should lead to a more democratic and accountable health service.
- Partnership with local communities can increase access to new sources of funding (Single Regeneration Budget, Joint Finance, charitable trusts, European Union etc.).

- It can help tackle barriers to access to services for marginalised groups and promote equity.
- It is vital to PCGs in developing their accountability to the public.

The question must be asked, however: Is participation empowering? Not necessarily – it will only be so if participation produces results and clear progress, and participants can then feel the power of their input. The medical model and professional 'expertise' serve to disempower.

COMMUNITY DEVELOPMENT

There is so much vagueness in terminology these days and community development has almost achieved mainstream acceptance, so it is important to be clear about what we mean by it. A community development approach is:

- concerned with powerlessness and disadvantage – sharing power, skills, knowledge and experience
- enables people to grow and change according to their own needs
- does not oppress or damage the environment
- aims to empower and enable those deprived of power
- nurtures collective action according to the community's agenda
- challenges individuals, policies and practices that discriminate unfairly against black people, women, people with disabilities, lesbians and gay men, older people and others disadvantaged by society.

Why should community development be central to Primary Care Group work with local communities? From our experience, community development will achieve the three latter points above, plus:

- engage with large numbers of people who live in disadvantaged communities
- strengthen communities and gradually build up capacity to ensure accountability and 'new approaches to governance'.

THE CHALLENGE: INEQUALITIES IN HEALTH IN NEWCASTLE

The West End of Newcastle is typical of many inner city estates. Its deprivation score worsened in all seven wards between the 1981 and 1991 censuses. There is high unemployment, low wage work and one third of all children are born into poverty. On average someone is almost twice as likely to die before the age of 65 in West City ward than in the rest of the North-East, and the North-East is worse than other regions.

The inverse-care law still operates: the West End PCG area has the highest rate of premature death from heart disease yet the lowest rate of access to hospital treatment for heart disease — although this is beginning to be addressed. Ethnic monitoring in Newcastle demonstrates discrimination in heart disease, diabetes, cancer and mental health care, there is little access for deaf people, and there are barriers for wheelchair users.

THE RESPONSE: COMMUNITY ACTION ON HEALTH 1995-99

The project uses a community development approach to participation in health issues, which goes beyond consultation and needs assessment in trying to develop the local communities' right to act on their own health agendas. A clear commitment to equity and challenging discrimination informs the community development approach.

After a consultation with the local community in 1994, the health authority and the locality group funded a community development work post that is accountable not to them but to the local community. The worker has visited an ever increasing number of local community groups and works with them to develop their health agenda and proposals for improvements in current services and for the development of new services where necessary. The focus is on networking and bringing together groups around common issues with the relevant health and social care services management, to push for the changes the community has identified as a priority.

The project informs local groups about the health services, and future developments and local views on health issues are documented in an annual report, which is then returned to the groups and forms the basis for future work. The work has actively sought to involve groups who are often particularly marginalised such as the black and ethnic minority communities, gay and lesbian groups, older people, adolescents and people with a physical and sensory disability. In some cases this has had clear resource implications, for instance the need to provide sign language interpreters for deaf people. Resources need to allow for the provision of crèches, carer support and language interpreters.

The 90-plus groups involved last year included tenants' associations, community sub-committees, luncheon clubs, parent-and-toddler groups, black voluntary sector projects and special interest groups such as the pensioner's association, the local deaf club and others. The work is entirely dependent on a vibrant grass-roots community development network of projects in the area.

There is an annual health conference attended by more than 200 people, where the year's proposals are prioritised by local people, with primary health staff and management in attendance. The community has nominated a group of local people called Community Action on Health to act on the issues raised and to give direction to the work of the development worker – this is the prime method for accountability of the worker to the local community.

Instead of advertising for a 'lay representative' the PCG has agreed that two representatives be elected through the Community Action on Health network and that they develop a form of community representation more accountable to the local community. The worker and members of Community Action on Health meet regularly with the Primary Care Group executive to explore ways of responding to and working with the communities' agenda, recognising the limitations of the PCG agenda to adequately deal with the wide range of community issues raised by the project.

New initiatives have developed from the work, many with the help of outside funding. These include the Youth Enquiry Service, a youth one-stop shop; the Families First project where local women have been trained to provide support for local families under stress; a community care development project seeking to meet local needs of elderly frail people and people with a disability, and a black counselling service.

A recent independent evaluation of the work highlighted the fact that a community development approach has been useful in engaging with a large number of local community groups and representatives and has created a systematic focus for the PCG on health inequalities and discrimination against minority groups. Professionals appreciate the project for its awareness-raising of minority group issues and a majority of them felt that it was a good use of health service funding. Community representatives felt that it had also helped them better understand the issues of discrimination against minority groups, as it was the first time that some of them had worked with disabled groups or black groups.

COMMUNITY PARTICIPATION IN PRIMARY CARE GROUPS AND THE HEALTH ACTION ZONE IN TYNE AND WEAR

There is now a network of continuing, supported, community involvement initiatives at PCG level across the Newcastle and North Tyneside district, influenced by the work in the West End. These community development projects are all coming together under the umbrella of Community Action on Health Newcastle. Four out of five PCGs now fund community development work. The Newcastle Health Partnership has adopted a strategy for community participation based on community development principles and has funded a city-wide co-ordination post. This is to create links between the different community development initiatives funded by the PCGs and to ensure the involvement of communities of interest in an emerging city-wide community action group. Links are being created between the communities of different districts in the Tyne and Wear Health Action Zone, and two 'Real Voices' conferences have been held to bring together communities from across the area and to establish their agenda.

Before embarking on community consultation, involvement or participation, PCGs should answer these questions:

1. Are you clear about what you are trying to achieve?
2. Are you aiming to consult or to involve ?
3. Does the approach allow people to have adequate information to inform their agenda?
4. Is the agenda set by professionals or by the community?
5. Is the approach top-down or bottom-up?
6. Are there mechanisms for ensuring that the decision-making process is open to community views and that there is feedback to the community?
7. Is the approach likely to involve a reasonable spread of people along age/gender/race/class lines (geographical community versus identity and interest communities)?
8. Are you distinguishing between the community and voluntary sectors?
9. If you are tackling inequalities, what communities will you prioritise?

Principles for involving the public

- The community is an asset and part of the solution, not a problem.
- Community representatives need support to link to the wider community, and community development input must be accountable to the local community and not the PCG.
- Any approach must involve marginalised minority groups – people with sensory or physical disability, gay men and lesbians, the black community etc.
- Financial support is necessary to ensure access — for a crèche, carer support, interpretation (including sign language), translation, audiotapes etc)
- Community participation strategies are required where the community can set the agenda and raise the issues of concern to them.
- To involve the public, PCGs need to be developed so that they are responsive to the community's view.
- The process is important, but if the community does not see some concrete outcomes for their voluntary involvement, they will lose interest.

- If meetings include local people they must be conducted to ensure their participation, and must avoid jargon.

POSTSCRIPT

Is anything fundamentally changing for the better for local people in marginalised communities and groups? Having seen City Challenge, five rounds of Single Regeneration Budget funding and now New Deal for Communities and Sure Start, I wonder if there is any real commitment to radically altering the tremendous level of social exclusion experienced by so many in this society.

Sir Herman Ouseley recently expressed the feeling that a great opportunity, post-Stephen Lawrence, was being squandered to do anything about racism in society and in the institutions of society. Equally, the struggle to tackle health inequalities and to develop community participation in health is still very much on the margins. The Health Action Zone initiative – the health initiative most close to community development principles – runs the risk of being a separate initiative that is not part of changing the way the whole system operates to tackle inequalities in health.

The predominance of the medical model remains difficult to challenge and high-tech medicine still soaks up most resources. Equally, the institutions we are trying to influence have been managing the many changes presented to them, often without any sign of themselves being open to change – we still rely on key allies.

In our working lives has there ever been a better opportunity to really change the way things work, and to really focus on tackling health inequalities? It is up to us all to push these opportunities to the limit, and it is essential that PCGs are in the forefront of efforts to engage their local communities in the struggle to tackle health inequalities, and to develop healthier communities for the next generation.

Responding to the needs of adults and children with diabetes

Andrew Kenworthy
Assistant director (planning), Bradford Health Authority
Project director, Bradford Health Action Zone

These are our experiences of trying to completely re-engineer Bradford's diabetes services, based on the views of local people with diabetes and local professionals, all working together.

Bradford is a first wave Health Action Zone (HAZ). This was a major event for us, as many of Bradford's health needs are closely linked to such issues as poor housing and unemployment. Some health problems, such as wheezing, are linked to damp housing.

Becoming a HAZ enabled all the main organisations in Bradford to come together to focus on how we could improve health, rather than looking separately at improving housing, waiting lists or regeneration for example. We were able to be innovative, and look very differently at how to pull services and packages together for local people.

If we look at death rates from coronary heart disease, incidence of diabetes, unemployment, poor housing – any of the indicators of social deprivation you care to name – all of the most deprived areas of Bradford are exactly the same. The level of diabetes, for example, is four times the national average in several of the most deprived areas, but in more affluent places like Ilkley it is almost half the national average. So in looking to develop services, particularly around diabetes, it is not around investing across the patch, it is about identifying how best we can target people locally.

Bradford has a culturally rich population and there is a large proportion of people of South Asian origin. They have a significantly higher prevalence of diabetes and it is important that services are planned appropriately.

When people talk about diabetes, they conjure up images of injections and of drugs. The general level of knowledge and awareness of the condition needs to improve.

In the health service, one evolving approach to planning services is to plan around primary care. How do we make services in primary care better? These services come in a number of different forms; we have, for example, a large number of single-handed practices, which can make the improvement of the quality and uniformity of services challenging. We also thought about how we could improve hospital services – in Bradford we had only a half-time dedicated consultant diabetologist.

It is estimated that there are 12,000 people in the Bradford district who are diagnosed as diabetic, and that there are a further 4,000 people with undiagnosed diabetes. Those who are presently undiagnosed may present later with blindness, gangrene of the limbs or renal failure and may turn up in the accident & emergency department. If they do not present at an early stage they may have significantly greater ill health.

The basic problem with the half-time consultant-based service was that people were waiting far too long for treatment. We had waiting lists when people needed to have almost instantaneous access to the service, and needed support and help.

The HAZ concept is about community involvement, and about using the community as the starting point for planning services. So in looking at diabetes, one of our major priorities was to start by talking to people in the community. One of the first things we had to recognise was that there are different kinds of people in the community, all of them with different needs, all of them living in different places. There are also a significant number of children with diabetes in the district, and we needed to find a way of hearing their views.

We had to recognise that diabetes does not only impact on the individual with diabetes but on his or her family and community as well; so we needed to look at how we would go about planning services for the whole community. A lot of carers and the immediate family would be directly influenced by people's experience.

And as people have different lifestyles, it is important that these are adequately reflected when designing any package of care. We need to understand how people live, what their major influences are, before we can design services.

Transport is a crucial issue in some areas. The film 'Rita, Sue and Bob Too' is set on an estate three miles from the centre of Bradford; but to reach any of the major hospital facilities from there, patients must catch two or three different buses. So we needed to take account of the physical layout of Bradford in designing services.

We were afraid that we would all fall on our face because the traditional means by which services are planned are very well entrenched within health and social care services. But our HAZ plan pointed a clear way forward – we consulted by holding four workshops, each involving approximately 100 people. Those 100 people included children with diabetes, who drew pictures of what would make their lives with diabetes easier. All the workshops started with the proposition that they had experience of diabetes in their lives and a question about what would improve their experience, and the experience of others in future years. Issues were identified by the children, and by the professionals.

One of the key issues which came up was benefits and the Benefits Agency. Professionals in hospital and primary care, often doctors and nurses, were spending a significant amount of time helping people to fill in benefit forms, and we asked why they were doing this. If we could sort out the benefits that would free up more clinical time and availability.

Each of the workshops split into small groups of about eight, covering the spectrum of people across Bradford who would come into contact with people with diabetes, ranging from voluntary agency support groups, people with diabetes themselves, immediate family, consultants, nurses, healthcare professionals, primary care, optometrists and nursing home staff.

We identified a phenomenal number of issues, and we asked Professor George Alberti, President of the Royal College of Physicians, to come and give support to the process and to help summarise the issues. We also went out of our way to involve the private sector – many of the local pharmaceutical companies and pharmacists in Bradford have massive resources that could be used to raise awareness of diabetes.

It is a difficult process to bring together consultants – the medical fraternity, the major power bases in planning services – on the one hand, and local communities and local people on the other. There was significant opposition from some of the traditional power bases. However, what came out was a pathway of care for people with diabetes significantly broader than anything the district had planned in the past.

We learnt that people wanted:
- better access to chiropody
- better care in nursing homes, where the symptoms of diabetes may be to do with wanting to go to the toilet; nursing home care was seen as something of a desert, and was highlighted as a priority
- better monitoring of glaucoma by local optometrists, so that we pick up people earlier
- more people in the community to help and advise on diet, in order that people with diabetes could make choices for themselves

- advice on drugs and alcohol for adolescents with diabetes (something that had not been picked up in the past)
- advice on how to make healthy meals, particularly for the South Asian population, whose diet is very rich; initiatives included holding cookery demonstrations locally
- all GPs to have a range of facilities available to make sure that they knew which patients had diabetes, so establishing a key diabetes register across the patch
- advice on benefits, so that people knew what benefits they were entitled to when they accessed services
- telephone support, to be able to talk to other people about diabetes.

We undertook this process because diabetes is a major cause of death in Bradford and a lot of people's lives are ruined by it. The major finding was the need for more local services, and as a result 17 local diabetes clinics have been established across primary care in Bradford. These are staffed by general practitioners specially trained in diabetes, and they now provide 50-60 per cent of diabetes care in Bradford.

The four conferences helped to guide and prioritise more than half-a-million pounds' worth of investment in mainstream services for diabetes in Bradford. Some of that is Health Action Zone money, but the majority of it is mainstream health service cash. The investment is not solely in healthcare. For example, we are trying to work with Morrison's, the supermarket, to provide better food labelling, with the Benefits Agency and with optometrists.

In conclusion, the scale of the agenda that came out from the conferences as a result of listening to children and to the community was far greater than the very narrow perspective we had had in the past about how to plan services.

Evaluation and community development

Andrew Leeming
Community development worker, Stockport Healthcare NHS Trust

I am not an expert in evaluation, just a community worker who struggles with evaluation and has tried to study it. Let me begin with an example of the complexity of evaluation. Two people in two semi-detached houses are both making a cup of tea and at the same time they discover they have no milk in the house. They both make a plan, which is to put on their coats, go to the local shop, buy a pint of milk, pour the milk in the cup, pour the tea, and drink the tea. One of them goes out, goes to the shop, comes back with the milk, makes the tea and drinks it. The plan went absolutely perfectly.

The other person makes exactly the same plan, but just outside the shop meets a friend, the friend asks, 'Are you free?' she says 'Yes' and the friend suggests the Italian restaurant up the road for a quick bite to eat. They have a wonderful time, and chat and learn about each other's lives, and it is a great night out, at the end of which they have a cup of coffee.

One completely fulfilled the plan, and if evaluated got 100 per cent, but actually the other had the better experience and a better outcome – and didn't match the plan at all. She never bought the pint of milk, never went back home and never drank the cup of tea she was making, but it was a much better outcome.

Why evaluate?
- to improve practice
- to spread good practice
- the satisfaction of knowing a job is well done
- to identify unplanned benefits
- to enhance the legitimacy of work
- to minimise waste of resources
- to assess whether the work is ethically justifiable
- it is good practice.

'The exciting aspect of evaluation is that at its best, it fuses retrospection (yesterday), with pause for reflection (making time to take stock of today), with renewal (increased confidence and motivation for tomorrow).' – R. de Groot (1996)

Why evaluate?
- funders demand it
- we want to know what works and what doesn't
- to help our planning
- to make the case for more money
- for those inside and outside the project to learn more about what we are doing – problems and strengths
- to see the full balanced picture, positive and negative
- to tell the story of the project
- so that we don't re-invent the wheel.

What do we evaluate?
- economy, efficiency and effectiveness, or any other variation of the three Es
- people's stories or testimonies
- quantitative versus qualitative evidence
- what is valued by the community, workers, bosses and others
- the aims of the project
- short, long and mid-term outcomes.

What should we consider?
- are we doing the right thing?
- are we doing the thing right?
- the project and staff
- effects of project work
- sustainability
- the process
- outcomes
- aims and objectives
- evaluation through the life of the project
- unexpected outcomes.

Who evaluates?
Workers, bosses, sponsors, independent external assessors, local people, those involved, everyone.

Who is involved, and why?

- an independent evaluator – are they objective?
(it depends who is paying them); for their technical expertise
- people running the project (service providers and development workers); for their in-depth knowledge, their commitment to improving the project, and to offer a learning process
- people who participate in the project; because on-going critical reflection is built into community development; it is also empowering
- funding agencies, to justify expenditure, and to inform future expenditure
- the wider community, to develop skills.

FOURTH GENERATION EVALUATION

The first generation is measurement generation; the evaluator is the technical expert, who administers appropriate tests and pronounces with authority the results and what it means. Professionals select the criteria.

The second generation is description or objective-orientated generation – the evaluator measures quality against measurable, stated objectives and outcomes, i.e. they are looking at strengths and weaknesses.

The third generation is judgement generation – the evaluator becomes the judge and retains the technical and descriptive functions of the first two generations. The evaluator decides what should be measured. There is an assumption that the evaluator is in the best position to evaluate.

Problems with these approaches are that all bias is the concern of the sponsor or manager; they cannot accommodate 'value pluralism' (there has to be a single measurable function that everyone subscribes to), and they are biased towards quantitative analysis and the discovery of the one 'true truth'.

Fourth generation evaluation is described as the interpretive generation, based on and guided by issues identified by stakeholders (a stakeholder is anyone with a stake in the project or service under evaluation). Guba and Lincoln[1] (1989) suggest that 'fourth generation moves beyond measurement – and just getting the facts – to include the myriad human, political, social, cultural and contextual elements that are involved'. It is useful in community development because it allows the range of actors within a project to describe what kind of information and criteria count as success or otherwise for them.

Rebien[2] suggests five advantages:

1. Failure to involve stakeholders is unfair and discriminatory
2. Evaluation produces information, and information is power; stakeholders must have access to that power.
3. Involvement facilitates the use of evaluation results.
4. Involvement broadens the perspective of evaluation and raises questions and answers that may not have been thought of.
5. Involvement facilitates mutual learning.

All stakeholders are allowed to raise claims (any assertion that is favourable to the person being evaluated), concerns (any assertion that is unfavourable) and issues (any state of affairs about which reasonable persons may disagree). This is then negotiated, then re-negotiated, then re-negotiated with new information until consensus, partial consensus or breakdown. This can go on and on and on. Fourth generation evaluation never stops, it merely pauses.

But it is not without problems:
- People can still dominate, assert legal claims, obligations and power issues
- Is the evaluator without 'baggage'?
- Can consensus be reached by polar opposites? Ever?
- Is participation by all possible, and do people want to participate?
- Results are not generalisable - they are only useful in the context they are produced.

ISSUES, BARRIERS, BOTTOM LINES AND SOLUTIONS

- There is no time to do evaluation
- There is too much writing about evaluation to read it all
- Lack of understanding of community development
- Only traditional models of evaluation are used
- The long-term nature of community development work
- Whose measurements do we use?
- How do you prove worth?
- We only evaluate around the edges in big organisations
- Pressure to prove effectiveness
- Is it acceptable to evaluate negatively ('look at this cock-up!')?
- Everyone is fighting for their own slice of the cake
- Do we or they know what to evaluate?
- Lack of control in a community development situation – we do not set the agenda
- How do you time evaluation?

- Other pressures in the organisation take over
- We urgently need quantifiable results, such as a decrease in mortality
- The public value expensive surgical operations, not the 'woolly' stuff of community development.
- What we evaluate is often affected by cost
- How do we bring out challenges (without threatening those being evaluated) so that we can learn from the experience and avoid replicating something that does not work?
- Can we be honest when something does not work, or will we been seen to have failed?

Solutions suggested by workshop participants included increasing people's understanding of community development, and opening up the debate.

This workshop was over-subscribed, which indicates the necessity to open up the debate. It may also indicate that evaluation is something with which many of us struggle.

Bibliography

1. Guba E and Lincoln Y (1989), Fourth Generation Evaluation. Sage, Newbury Park
Leeming A (1999), Community Development and Evaluation: Moving towards a model of cohabitation.
Unpublished, Sheffield Hallam University
2. Rebien CC (1996), Participatory Evaluation of Development Assistance. Dealing with power and facilitative learning. Evaluation Vol.2 No.2. April 1996. p151-171

Cotmanhay Action Group

Jenny Mellor
Community health visitor, South Derbyshire Community Health Services
NHS Trust

Cotmanhay Action Group is a community group that represents the electoral wards of Ilkeston North and Cotmanhay in south Derbyshire. The area is identified as having a high level of deprivation, after the demise of the coal mining and steel industries. The group was initially set up by the community health visitor and is open to anyone who has an interest in benefiting the area.

The aim of the group is 'to identity the needs of Cotmanhay residents and give them power to enhance their well-being'. The objectives are:
- to hold open meetings, where anyone who has an interest in the area is welcome to voice their ideas and opinions to the benefit of the area
- to encourage all agencies and local people to actively work together for the benefit of the area
- to formulate an action plan based on evidence gathered from the local community.

There are now over 60 people on the mailing list, and a mixture of residents and workers attend meetings. In its first year the group worked hard to develop a shared philosophy. This is enshrined in its constitution, and enhances partnership working.

The group's projects include:
- Cotmanhay Community Purchasing Scheme: a project run by residents for residents, enabling local people to get easy access to fresh, cheap fruit and vegetables.
- Cotmanhay Cover Up Campaign: a project aimed at raising awareness of the dangers of exposure to the sun. This project involves all the local junior school age children, school nurses, the community health visitor, environmental health officers, Erewash Borough Council, the school governors and all school staff.
- Cotmanhay Community Survey: the development process of this project in itself will increase social capital, because the aim of the survey is to involve as many local people as possible.
- Healthy Living Centre: we are developing a bid for a Healthy Living Centre, which will

be owned and run by the community, working in co-operation with statutory and other agencies.

These are just a flavour of some of the initiatives we are developing, but the most important aspect of our work is the development process itself, which is aimed at being open, honest, and inclusive. We respect each individual for who and what they are, and value every person's contribution.

PART THREE

What support/resources do communities need to participate more actively?

Is social capital a mediating structure for effective community-based health promotion?

Dr Marshall Kreuter
Distinguished scientist – service fellow, Division of Adult and Community Health,
National Center for Chronic Disease Prevention and Health Promotion
Centers for Disease Control and Prevention, USA

During most of my career, I have been interested in trying to better understand what it takes to plan, implement and evaluate community-based approaches to heath promotion. Since the early work on the cardiovascular disease prevention trials in the early Seventies, the terms 'community' and 'community-based' have become virtual shorthand for the basic tenets of health promotion.[1]

Grounded in principles of collaboration and participation, community-based health promotion has matured and become more robust over the past two decades. Practitioners and researchers are well aware that the actions we take, and the policies we develop, are strongly influenced by the environment, infrastructure and social norms where people live and work.

Even the most casual examination of problems like infant mortality, diabetes, HIV infection, teen smoking, violence and unplanned pregnancies quickly reveals the connections between those problems and their social and economic determinants – poverty, housing, and education. Furthermore, these social determinants, or risk conditions, tend to cluster by neighbourhood or community.[2, 3]

DO COMMUNITY-BASED APPROACHES WORK?

There is good news and not-so-good news about community-based approaches. The good news is that in addition to their compelling philosophical and intuitive appeal, there are numerous published studies that not only provide documentation that community-based health promotion programmes can yield positive effects, but that also delineate the salient theories, processes, and methods that seem to be associated with community-based health promotion programmes that work.[4, 5, 6, 7 8, 9, 10]

That's the good news. The not-so-good news is that the ratio of successful to not-so-successful programmes is disappointing – typical of what you will find in the literature is an assessment of the effectiveness of community-based health promotion carried out by Hancock, Sanson-Fisher and their colleagues published in the American Journal of Preventive Medicine in 1992. They reported mixed and somewhat equivocal results, even for some programmes where it seemed apparent that appropriate standards for planning and implementation had been applied and funding was allotted for the intervention.[11, 12]

In 1997, the Health Services and Resources Administration (HRSA) commissioned Nicole Lezin, Laura Young and myself to carry out a literature review to address the question: Do collaboratives and consortia lead to changes in health status or systems change? Based on our analysis of about 100 published articles describing the use of collaboratives to attain either health or system change effects, we came to a conclusion not dissimilar to that of Hancock and others: some programmes do yield definitive outcomes, but the ratio of success is disappointing.

Specifically, our analysis led us to conclude that:
1. There is a gross underestimation of the time and complexity of a collaborative effort.
2. People have unrealistic expectations about what a collaboration can do (dose response).
3. The absence of a sound theory framework and logic model for evaluating community-based health promotion may mean that changes are going undetected.

I suspect that all of us in health promotion have at least one thing in common, our mission: to promote health and prevent disease; and, to the extent we are successful, quality of life will be strengthened as well. I bring this matter of mission up for several reasons. First, public health can be tedious and sometimes, in the day-to-day trappings of our work, we lose sight of our goal. When, figuratively speaking, we lose our compass we can count on the fact that feelings of frustration and anxiety won't be far behind. So staying focused has some personal pay-offs. Second, the public we serve and the policy-makers whose decisions determine resource allocations for disease prevention and health promotion are entitled to know the extent to which our work is leading to health improvement. This, at least in part, is why there is so much fervour about the notion of 'evidence' vis a vis disease prevention and health promotion.

That said however, we should not be driven to seek 'evidence' just because it will keep the cost-effectiveness hounds at bay. As responsible practitioners and researchers we need valid indicators, 'evidence', to help us understand how we are doing and the extent to which we are making progress toward our goals.

This is all to say that being attracted to the concept of social capital is one thing, translating it into something that is linked to the goal of health improvement and subject to some reasonable measure of scrutiny is another. The late Geoffrey Rose, the distinguished British public health scholar, brilliantly declared the challenge for this kind of study in his book, A Strategy of Preventive Medicine. Acknowledging that social conditions and circumstances profoundly affect the lives and health of individuals, Rose asked, could these conditions be important in their own right? He wrote:

'There is a characteristic "hostility," or "aggression," which can be measured in individuals and which relates to their individual behaviour. What does the average hostility score of a population signify? Is it the propensity to internal or external aggression? And how does it differ between populations and cultures? What factors determine these differences? ... Can such characteristics of populations be changed, or can they only be passively observed? In principle, all of these questions should be and could be the subject of research'(p.63).[13]

SOCIAL CAPITAL

We define social capital as those specific processes among people and organisations, working collaboratively in an atmosphere of trust, that lead to accomplishing a goal of mutual social benefit.[14] Essentially, the theory of social capital suggests that collective actions requiring collaborative efforts are mediated by existing levels of trust, civic participation, social engagement and organisational co-operation.

Robert Putnam suggested that the core elements of social capital – trust and co-operation – could be developed over time by repeated interaction of people involved in long-term relationships that are supported by community institutions. Similarly, James Coleman, who formally introduced 'social capital' into sociological theory, argued that social capital has the potential to produce a stronger social fabric because it builds bonds based upon information, trust and solidarity between people, most often as by-products of other activities.[15] In virtually all conceptualisations of social capital, trust emerges as an especially salient factor. Pragmatically, it is important to note that Putnam suggests that the two key elements of social capital (trust and co-operation) are learned behaviours and are, by definition, amenable to change.

In our study, we made the assumption that the level of social capital in a community would be manifested in the variable presence or absence of four measurable constructs: trust, civic involvement, social engagement and reciprocity, where:

- Trust is the belief that an individual, group, or organisation can be relied upon to act in a consistent, fair, rational, and expected manner.
- Civic involvement is participation in activities that directly or indirectly contribute to a community's overall well-being. These include solitary activities such as voting or newspaper readership, as well as interactive activities, e.g. joining organisations that have civic improvement agendas.
- Social engagement refers to the interactions that foster connections among community members or organisations.
- Reciprocity refers to the expectation of a return on one's investment – the faith that an action or good deed will be returned in some form in the future.

Keeping in mind that our primary interest was to gain a better understanding of the forces that influence the effectiveness of community-based health promotion efforts, we posed these questions:

1. Can social capital be feasibly measured at the community level?
2. Can variations in social capital be detected at the community level?
3. If social capital can be feasibly measured, is there any evidence that variance in levels of social capital is associated with health promotion effectiveness?
4. If social capital can be measured and found to be associated with the effectiveness of health promotion programmes, can it be created or modified?

Our study addressed the first two questions.

METHODOLOGY

To estimate levels of social capital within potential target communities, the following procedure was tested as part of this protocol. Senior officials in a Midwestern health department were contacted and agreed to be participants and facilitators in the study. The theory of social capital and its operational constructs were presented and reviewed by the officials. They were then asked to designate communities that were either high or low in social capital. When the matter of common demographic characteristics was taken into account, two communities were left in the 'high' social capital cluster, and four remained in the 'low' category cluster. We considered this judgement to represent what we refer to as prima facie social capital. Contact was made with the local health officers in each of the remaining communities to ascertain which communities would be willing to participate in a research project to measure social capital. All agreed. Ultimately two communities with similar demographics were chosen, one with high and one with low prima facie social capital.

In an effort to confirm the prima facie estimate of social capital, three data sources were triangulated:

1. structured interviews with key informants and community leaders within each community
2. structured interviews with 10 county co-operative extension agents who served as external observers
3. a content analysis assessing the constructs of social capital reported in selected newspapers within the two communities.

Face to face structured interviews were conducted with 30 community stakeholders in each of the two study communities. The stakeholders, identified by the directors of the local health department in each community, consisted of persons recognised as community leaders representing the following sectors: business, health, news media, the faith community, social and health services (private, public, and voluntary), and local government. In addition to the 25 community stakeholders, the majority of the questions in the structured interview guide were also asked of five co-operative development workers from the two counties in which the communities were located.

The content analysis was quantitative. Front page and editorial articles were read and coded, based on the presence or absence of mentions of the four social capital constructs, and code counts for each construct in each paper were generated. The analysis of data generated from these three assessments was used to ascertain whether the selected communities varied in their respective levels of social capital in the direction predicted by the prima facie estimates.

To assess individual levels of social capital, a quantitative questionnaire was designed, using a modification of the protocol recommended by Windsor and his colleagues.[16] First, a pool of 40 questions was created. These questions were linked conceptually to the four constructs of social capital and were either based on previous questionnaires or on theoretical assumptions underlying social capital. Measurement examples frequently cited in the literature include: voter turnout, newspaper readership, the number of social action groups and youth groups in an area, day care centres in a community, perceptions of trust in institutions and people, personal commitment to the common good, and the perceived strength of social networks in families.

A panel of international experts in the fields of behavioural science and health promotion was convened to review and critique the questions.[17] Additions, deletions and revisions were then made based on the consultants' recommendations. These collective steps provided a level of consensual validity for the content of the questionnaire.[18]

After field testing, the scale was administered, using random digit dialing, to 400 respondents (18 years or older) in each community.

Figure 1 provides a schematic outline of the research design used in this study. The triangles marked A and B connote the combined findings through triangulation from structured interviews with community leaders and county co-operative development workers, and a newspaper content analysis in the two study towns. Findings from telephone surveys in the two communities are labelled C and D. A comparison of data from A and B addresses the first research question, verifying differing levels of prima facie social capital. It also reveals perceptions of social capital at the organisational level in the two communities.

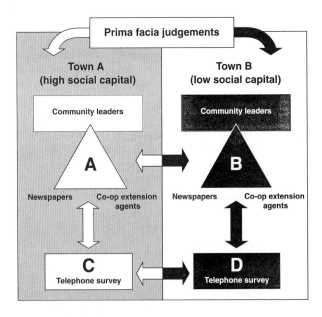

Figure 1 Two-community pilot study design

Comparison of A with C and of B with D addressed the second research question: whether the population-level measure of social capital reflected the prima facie and organisational-level assessments of social capital.

In general, the data triangulation used to verify prima facie estimates of social capital confirmed the hypothesized difference between communities. Interview data from community leaders and co-operative extension agents provided the strongest confirmatory evidence for different levels of social capital between communities. Although evidence from the newspaper content analysis was less confirmatory, there was a statistically significant difference confirming the prima facie estimate for the construct of trust. Comparison of findings from the data triangulation and the telephone survey was the primary method used to assess telephone survey validity.

FINDINGS

Qualitative interviews revealed rich information about the quality and quantity of social capital in the two communities we studied:

- sources of social capital – government, religious institutions, personal relationships
- uses of social capital – securing human capital and financial capital to solve community problems
- factors that facilitate social capital – normative traditions, positive history, homogeneity
- barriers to social capital – history (preoccupation with past failures, hanging on to a negative past), social/economic change and a general pessimism and sense of doubt.

One of the central questions we were exploring was: If the level of social capital in a given community were known, would the mean responses to a valid social capital questionnaire, administered to a random sample of a community's population, serve as a proxy indicator of the known level of social capital in that community?

As I previously mentioned, we had theorised that the results from the population surveys carried out in each community would mirror the results from the triangulation analysis of organisational social capital assessment in the same community. That didn't happen. The survey results from both communities were generally positive and there were no statistically significant differences between the two communities on any of the constructs.

Let me offer two possible explanations for this finding: first, the population questionnaire may have consisted of items that were not sufficiently discriminating. Recall the procedure we used: (1) content validity confirmed by the expert panel, (2) the majority of the items used in the questionnaire had been adapted from previously published and tested instruments, and (3) confirmation by those administering the telephone interviews that the process was going smoothly with no indication of confusion among interviewers or respondents.

In retrospect, these criteria may have been insufficient. More extensive pretesting of the instrument, possibly including a cognitive assessment, may have eliminated this problem prior to survey administration. Observations by Tourangeau and Rasinski[19] provide added perspective on this issue. They note that when individuals are asked to respond to attitude questions using an attitude framework that they rarely access or that is not strongly formed, strong context effects and measurement error are introduced.

The towns selected for this study are stable communities with rich cultural histories. Visitors to the two towns, frequenting local shops and restaurants, would discover the residents to be friendly, pleasant and engaging; they would probably notice nothing unusual about either community. From a pragmatic perspective, residents of these two towns are likely to hold positive perceptions about social capital operating in their communities since they may have little frame of reference to make decisions about the constructs being assessed.

On the other hand, community leaders, actively involved in the day-to-day operation of community organisations and government, must continually adjust their attitudes about social capital based on experiences of interacting with other leaders and their respective organisations.

Thus, it may be that measures of social capital at the population level require that questions be framed within the context of a specific issue, rather than the more general approach used in the present study. For example, Raudenbush et al examined the association between a dimension of social capital (community efficacy) in a neighbourhood setting with a specific dependent variable, youth violence.[20] At a minimum, this raises concerns about the universality of social capital constructs.

A second possible explanation for the lack of association between the results of structured interviews with community leaders and those from the telephone survey is that organisational-level social capital and population social capital may represent two different dimensions of social capital and/or that the existence of organisational social capital may be independent of personal/individual levels of social capital.

SOME FINAL THOUGHTS

The approach we used to assess organisational social capital was time-consuming, tedious and not cheap. Nevertheless, I believe we have provided reasonably strong evidence that at least what we are calling organisational social capital is indeed amenable to measurement and this initial work provides at least a portion of a foundation to build upon. I am confident that we (the collective we) can create a more refined and efficient mechanism to assess organisational level social capital.

If the pattern of variability we found is evident elsewhere, we will be able to offer private and public sector funders the evidence that will enable them to make more informed decisions about the ways to infuse health-related funding into a given community. That could be done either by earmarking resources to build the capacity that is requisite for successful interventions, or, armed with the evidence that such capacity is already in place, by allocating resources directly to the interventions themselves.

Now a word about future directions. Other researchers in this area are finding assessments of individual social capital to be complex and not too fruitful. Gerry Veenstra from the University of British Columbia in Vancouver had experienced similar difficulties in assessing social capital at the population level. And it isn't just the methodological difficulty (which I can assure you is huge) that is of concern.
I am afraid that a preoccupation with individual or even family level social capital runs the risk of being perceived as attacking the symptom ('you people need to be more co-operative and cohesive') instead of the problem (the systems and structures that, albeit unwittingly, compromise and sometimes conspire against basic social and economic needs).

My experiences lead me to agree with those who view social capital as a collective asset; as a feature of communities, rather than the property of an individual. As such, if I were asked how to expand the direction of social capital research, my response would be somewhat counter-intuitive. I would encourage us to move to engage those who control the power and resources. That is, using the constructs of social capital as a means to purposefully engage governments and businesses in actions designed to accomplish goals of mutual social benefit.

A second danger of focusing too much on individual and family level social capital has been identified by James Morone, a professor of political science at Brown University in the US. Ten years ago he wrote a book entitled The Democratic Wish, subtitled 'Popular participation and the limits of American government.[21] The central thesis of this book is that historically, Americans have always been committed to limiting the role of government, especially the central government.

He describes how this attitude began with the American Revolution wherein hastily organised committees grabbed political power away from British governors sent to rule over the colonies. He says that the notion of local empowerment is the 'central image' of the democratic wish, which he defines as 'the direct participation of a united people pursuing a shared communal interest, sceptical of central authority' – a definition with many of the characteristics of social capital.

I found Morone's insights instructive because, in reality, I am a hopeless idealist who is ashamed of our global disregard for social justice, and who is easily seduced by words like participation, teamwork and empowerment. Like Odysseus' song of the sirens, the language of democracy is seductive. But Morone reminds us of the obvious: behaving democratically is hard stuff. It is like collaboration, which appears to be an unnatural act among consenting adults! It is painful. It means giving up things we value as individuals for the benefit of the group.

But what I found most intriguing about his thesis is his concern that, while it is true that a central component of democracy, at least democracy in America, is an inherent scepticism for and rebelling against central authority, we run the risk of carrying that too far and setting up 'either or' options, in effect, framing the government as the enemy.

Think of it for a moment in our own field. It is ahistorical not to acknowledge the huge human benefits that have been realised by smallpox eradication, child and adult immunisation, sanitation, nutrition, and by highway and traffic safety initiatives, most of which were launched as centrally supported initiatives. Shortly we will see the eradication of dracunculiasis (guinea worm disease) and it will be due in large part to global collaboration involving a combination of central governments, businesses and localities. So, embracing and educating the sources of influence and power is one of our great opportunities and challenges. Our ability to make the concept of social capital tangible and coherent may help us in that challenge.

In short, can we measure social capital? We think so. Our work is admittedly cumbersome and, in some ways, crude. But, there is no question in my mind that we can measure it.

Can we modify social capital? I think that there is considerable evidence that organisations can change and businesses certainly think so – why are there so many respected firms with specialities in organisational change? Furthermore, our own literature review on the small wins, aggregated over time, can solidify and sustain a process, not a specific programme (I am not sure we want to sustain a programme the value of which has run its course) that, over time, nurtures healthy communities.

Bibliography

1. Green LW & Kreuter MW (1999), Health Promotion Planning: An Ecological and Educational Approach. Mountain View, CA: Mayfield Publishing, 2nd edition.

2. Evans RG, Barer ML, Barer, Marmor TR (1994), Why Are Some People Healthy And Others Not? The Determinants of Health in Populations. New York: Aldine de Gruyter.

3. Gerstein R, Labelle J, MacLeod S, et al (1991), Nurturing Health: A Framework on the Determinants of Health. Toronto, ON: Premier's Council on Health Strategy.

4. I have purposely used the phrase 'programmes that work' rather than efficacy, because in public health parlance, the latter implies a precise level of outcome that is often unrealistic for community-based interventions. See: Fishbein M (1996), 'Great Expectations, or Do We Ask Too Much from Community-Level Interventions?' American Journal of Public Health, 86(8): 1075-1076.

5. Kotchen JM, McKean HE, Jackson-Thayer S, et al (1987), 'The Impact of a High Blood Pressure Control Programme on Hypertension Control and CVD Mortality'. JAMA, 257: 3382-3386.

6. Centers for Disease Control (1991), Increasing Breast Cancer Screening Among the Medically Underserved, Dade County, FL. MMWR, 40(16): 261-263.

7. Puska P, et al (1985), 'The Community-based Strategy to Prevent Coronary Heart Disease: Conclusions From the Ten Years of the North Karelia Project'. Annual Review of Public Health, 6: 147-193.

8. Vartiainen E, et al (1986), 'Prevention of Non-communicable Diseases: Risk Factors in Youth – the North Karelia Youth Project (1984-1988)'. Health Promotion, 1(3): 269-283.

9. Lando HA, Loken B, Howard-Pitney B, Pechacek T (1990), 'Community Impact of a Localized Smoking Cessation Contest'. American Journal of Public Health, 80: 601-603.

10. Pierce JP, Macaskill P, Hill A (1990), 'Long-Term Effectiveness of Mass Media Led Antismoking Campaigns in Australia'. American Journal of Public Health, 80: 565-569.

11. Hancock L, Sanson-Fisher R, Redman S, et al (1992), 'Community Action for Health Promotion: A Review of Methods and Outcomes'. American Journal of Preventive Medicine, 13: 229-239

12. 'The COMMIT Research Group. Community Intervention Trial for Smoking Cessation (COMMIT)II: Changes in Adult Cigarette Smoking Prevalence'. American Journal of Public Health, 85: 183-192. A community-based health promotion strategy meets standards for planning and implementation when it: (1) adheres to sound theories of community engagement and participation, (2) employs methods that are grounded in sound theory and have been shown to be effective in similar settings, (3) addresses the socio-political system as well as environmental and behavioural forces that influence health, (4) is managed by capable, competent staff, (5) has adequate financial, administrative and organisational support, and (6) is deemed appropriate vis a vis the problem, circumstances and audience in question.

13. Rose G (1992), The Strategy of Medicine. Oxford: Oxford University Press.

14. This interpretation incorporates Coleman's emphasis upon social relations within and among organisations and structures that are built up by people themselves. It also highlights Putnam's notion of mutual interest. See Coleman J (1990), Foundations of Social Theory. Cambridge, MA: Harvard University Press. See also Putnam RD (1993), 'The Prosperous Community: Social Capital and Public Life'. The American Prospect, 13: 33-42.

15. Coleman J & Hoffer T (1987), Public and Private High Schools: The Impact on Communities. New York: Basic Books.

16. Windsor RA, Baranowski T, Clark N, Cutter G (1984), Evaluation of Health Promotion Programmes. Mountain View, CA: Mayfield Publishing, 205-212.

17. The expert panel consisted of LW Green, B Baker, D Cotton, R Goodman, P Gillies, M Kelly, D McQueen, D Higgins, R Levinson, G Veenstra.

18. Green LW & Lewis FM (1986), Measurement and Evaluation in Health Education and Health Promotion. Mountain View, CA: Mayfield Publishing, 106.

19. Tourangeau R & Rasinski KA (1988), 'Cognitive Processes Underlying Context Effects in Attitude Measurement'. Psychological Bulletin, 103(3), 299-314.

20. Sampson RJ, Raudenbush SW and Earle F (1997), 'Neighbourhoods and Violent Crime, A Multilevel Study of Collectiev Efficacy', Science 277, 918-924

21. Morone JA (1990), The Democratic Wish, Basic Books

Old Trafford Community Development Project

Emma Bates
Co-ordinator, Old Trafford Community Development Project

The area of Old Trafford in Trafford, Greater Manchester is a real area where people live, not just one huge football ground; in fact the Manchester United stadium is not even in Old Trafford. The area includes two electoral wards, Clifton and Talbot, with a total population of about 13,000. We are about a mile out of the city centre, bordering Moss Side to the East and Hale and Bowden in Cheshire to the South, so Trafford is a very varied borough, which has led to Old Trafford being neglected for a long time.

The area has a varied population. The Clifton ward breaks down into about 18.6 per cent Black groups, 21.9 per cent South Asian groups, and 4.9 per cent Chinese, Polish and other groups and the remainder white. The 1991 census said that we had 27 first languages in our local primary school, a figure that is now likely to be out of date.

The highest level of long-term limiting illness in the borough, 15.9 per cent, is in Clifton, where they also have the highest standardised mortality ratio.

Only 16 per cent of pupils gained five or more GCSEs, compared with a borough-wide average of 54 per cent. Unemployment, particularly long-term unemployment, is high and many of the people who have been long-term unemployed are still not tapping into opportunities in the regeneration process such as training schemes and the local job shop. Youth unemployment is also higher in our end of the borough, which is a key factor in the social exclusion of local young people. Incidentally, the area recently gained Single Regeneration Budget 5 (SRB5) funding approval, to be used for improving opportunities for young people in the Old Trafford and Gorsehill areas. The level of school exclusions and non-attendance is a challenge for all of us, if we are to help some of those young people access job opportunities.

Other issues are crime and fear of crime, poverty, low pay and poor quality jobs, and a poor physical environment. Higher levels of mental distress and anxiety were found in

Old Trafford in a study about three years ago, and that is much higher for the Black and South Asian populations, largely because of racism and isolation.

One of Old Trafford's assets is its cultural mix. It is a very exciting place to live. There is community spirit that is perhaps absent in more suburban areas. That is not to say that it all joins up; but in some neighbourhoods there is quite a strong community spirit. There are also a lot of skills and expertise, and many people have been involved in unpaid community work for years.

We want to ensure that links are made with health, as part of the wider regeneration process, so that people can see the links between the different statutory organisations; this is partly about more effective partnership working.

Many organisations are still not comfortable using the word 'poverty', but it is important in any regeneration process to measure poverty and what is happening around that. Outputs are being monitored in many of the funding regimes, but that does not necessarily tell us about the quality of people's lives.

Where there are jobs being created they are not necessarily well paid, and many of them are insecure. We also have postcode discrimination, with some employers binning application forms from an M16 address. That is an issue that goes beyond community development, and one that our partner agencies are seeking to tackle.

We are pushing for the use of local labour in the regeneration process. There are many unemployed labourers in Old Trafford, yet when the contract for some housing improvement work was let, the gangs were initially coming in from Liverpool and Birmingham. We put an article about this on the front page of our community newspaper, and steps have now been taken to ensure that a certain percentage of local people are employed.

We have no full-time nursery provision, which is having a knock-on effect on other aspects of regeneration. People are seeking to bring jobs and training courses into the area, but the lack of full-time nursery provision means that women in particular cannot access them.

We have a mix of housing stock, ranging from back-to-back Coronation Street-type housing, high- and low-rise flats, through to owner-occupied houses; there are six council estates, a number of housing associations, and a growing number of private landlord properties, split into bedsits. There has been improvement in some parts of the area, but there are estates with very poor insulation, damp infestation, even gaps at the bottom of people's walls. It is hard for people to maintain their gardens because they cannot afford garden equipment, or they have nowhere to store the equipment because they live in very small houses.

The concerns of people from ethnic minorities have been neglected for a long time, which has created tensions around community development work and priorities.

Old Trafford Community Development was set up three years ago, having been talked about for probably six or seven years before that. The idea came from local people, rather than through the beginning of the regeneration work. At that time there was very poor community involvement in the SRB Round 1 process. But things have moved a long way forward since then and the organisations now have a real commitment to involving local people, although there is still some learning to do. Cynicism was high, and does not change overnight. Even now, although things are moving forward, and there is a commitment to listening to local people's needs, some people still ask how it will make a difference to them, complain that it is just another strategy that will simply sit on a shelf, or say that there are a lot of highly paid workers talking about things that will make no difference to local people's lives.

Old Trafford Community Development is a voluntary organisation. Local ownership is central to the organisation, so the management committee is 70 per cent local people. Partner organisations such as the Training and Enterprise Council (TEC), the council, the health authority and the private sector also sit on the management committee — which has its pros and cons. All the staff are local residents, which also has advantages and disadvantages.

When we started three years ago we identified initial priorities by speaking to all the different local community groups, and it has grown from there. We were involved with various aspects of needs assessment work, in particular on an estate to the west of the Old Trafford area, which had been cut off from the wider regeneration, so we trained two local residents to carry out qualitative research with us. We are now analysing that, and hope that it will feed into the wider regeneration and that the estate will be included. We intend to use millennium events, and long-term investment in the community, to celebrate what is going on in Old Trafford.

We are concerned to increase people's involvement in decision-making processes and forums, and part of that is about supporting local community and voluntary groups. They are the people who the large organisations contact for consultation, so it is important that they work effectively. We have been doing training needs analysis and providing various training courses, helping them to engage with the organisations and to understand how to access the local authority and the health authority.

We have been doing some long-term confidence building training with residents who said they did not go to meetings, or did not speak at meetings, because they lacked confidence. Even though they are a small group there have been some real changes in the people who have been involved.

We have set up a database about the community and its voluntary organisations, and other organisations in the area, to help people make the most of local resources; this is available to organisations and residents. It provides local information and advice, from the health authority phoning up to inquire about the languages in the area to somebody coming into the office to ask if their house is to be done up. We are providing training about funding sources for the community and voluntary sector and helping groups to engage in the various bidding processes. At the moment we are awash with Health Action Zones, Healthy Living Centres and Education Action Zones.

We have a high proportion of young people in Old Trafford, and we want to help the youth organisations to work together, make the most of their resources and pool their buildings and equipment.

We are also involved in communication. The community newspaper has been very important. We have helped to co-ordinate local people to run the Old Trafford News, which goes to every household, shop and office in the area. Local residents form the editorial group and local residents deliver it. Its aims are threefold: to increase the positive profile of Old Trafford, by helping people to see some of the good things about Old Trafford and get away from some of the stigma; second, it is about giving local people a voice, and helping them to speak about their needs and concerns, and third, it is an opportunity for the organisations to communicate their information.

Until the paper started, there were people who did not know that there was a play centre around the corner or that there was a youth club down the road. The opportunity for people to write in and use it as a voice has been an important learning opportunity for residents and organisations. If we can increase that communication, we hope that both sides will start to listen to each other more. We have also developed a youth page, giving an opportunity for young people to write about their concerns. It has also been an opportunity to work with sections of the Black community. There were a number of individuals who wanted to write for the paper, but did not feel that they had the confidence or the skills, so we started a Black writers' workshop. The further funding has enabled us to consult on how to ensure the Black perspective is present throughout the project.

We have two very underused parks in the area, because of fear of crime, despite the fact that most people do not have gardens, so we are hoping to increase activities in the parks to increase the feeling of safety there, in partnership with Groundwork Trust. We are also involved in setting up a loan scheme for garden tools and equipment.

One of the major blocks to community initiative in the area is the lack of building space. We are surrounded by derelict buildings, but there is a lot of initiative among local people, and we are working with the local authority voluntary and community organisations to find a base.

Some of the challenges for the future arise from our local ownership. Yes, we have 70 per cent local involvement in the management committee, but it does not all go swimmingly. Some of the tensions around community development as a whole can be played out in the management committee, and working towards local people steering the project is an ongoing issue. There are also tensions between different parts of the community represented on the management committee, for instance between certain cultural groups.

It would be much easier for us to be run by the local authority or the health authority, which could do all the management, but we would not have the same local ownership. Helping people to develop competencies and skills is part of what community development is about in Old Trafford. There are also issues around sustainability: we have just got over that first hurdle of going beyond the three-year stage, but as all voluntary organisations know, the future is often uncertain. And that is not good for community development.

Amber Valley Partnership Quality of Life Action Group:
Somercotes Needs Assessment Project

Mary Hague
Public health strategy co-ordinator, Amber Valley Borough Council

Roberta Masters
Superintendent physiotherapist, Community Health Services Trust

Sarah Laman
Co-ordinator, Fleet Arts

First, some background about the Amber Valley Partnership organisation. It involves agencies from the private, public and voluntary sectors, including the Southern Derbyshire Health Authority, Amber Valley Borough Council, the newly formed primary care groups, Derbyshire County Council (including the youth service, education and social services), business, the Council for Voluntary Service, voluntary groups and community groups such as tenants' and residents' associations, mums and tots and similar groups, and arts groups. And, very importantly, the people of Amber Valley.

The Quality of Life Action Group is a subgroup of the Amber Valley Partnership. Its aim is to improve the health and quality of life of people throughout Amber Valley, particularly through partnership working and tackling the underlying factors that impact on health and well-being. We use a definition of health which recognises the impact of factors such as poor housing, poverty, and other socio-economic and environmental factors.[1]

The Quality of Life Action Group has been commissioned to devise a health strategy. The development of this strategy involved the opinions of many different people and was quite an undertaking, because agencies and individuals came with their own agendas. Eventually the strategy developed as a document covering three years, a document which is very flexible and open to change as things develop.[2]

Key aims include:

- to make improvements in the underlying social, economic and environmental causes of ill health
- to provide opportunities for all people in Amber Valley to take greater control in improving their quality of life
- to ensure that each partner will contribute to the improvement of health and life quality through partnership working, and to strengthen and develop those relationships between the partnership agencies.

In addition to those aims, the strategy has guiding principles. One particularly important guiding principle is that organisations should strive to work with individuals and communities to develop a shared responsibility.

From this health strategy, each agency in the Quality of Life Action Group is currently submitting its own action plans, which are being collated to fulfil the strategy, aims and objectives, and to help provide a more co-ordinated approach to health improvement in Amber Valley.

Amber Valley is a semi-urban rural area in Derbyshire. A major problem in Amber Valley is access, whether it be access to services because of transport, or access to information. This is why our health strategy works towards a more co-ordinated approach that will identify gaps, whether it be in provision for older people, or geographical groups, or any other issue.

Amber Valley is a very mixed area. There are recognised areas of poverty such as Somercotes, particularly on the eastern side of Amber Valley. Access to information and to services is an issue for Somercotes; there is also high unemployment, poor housing and lack of things to do, for young people and older people. Data from Southern Derbyshire Health Authority for Somercotes shows a link between rates of death from major diseases and the high unemployment and other socio-economic issues faced by Somercotes.[3]

THE SOMERCOTES NEEDS ASSESSMENT PROJECT

The aims of the project were, first, to identify factors affecting the health and quality of life of Somercotes people, using 'health' and 'quality of life' in the widest sense, and therefore developing a long-term sustainable approach to the improvement of health and quality of life.

Second, the project aimed to work with local people, using their local knowledge to offer solutions to local problems. Professionals within the Quality of Life Group identified Somercotes as an area to work in, so we could argue that it was initiated from the top down. But there was also a bottom-up approach, because the work to gather this information about Somercotes was done with local people, who devised questionnaires and other ways of to find out the issues, and ultimately to devise solutions.

A third aim was to fully involve local people so that they will influence future decisions and become actively involved in future developments. This links to community development, which is about ownership, about the individual saying what is wrong with their community and having the opportunity to influence future decision-making to improve the situation.

As the Somercotes Needs Assessment Project comes to an end, residents in Somercotes have formed the Somercotes Community Group. and started a breakfast club, because of concerns about childcare for children before school, and levels of nutrition.

In summer 1998 it was decided that an outside agency should be a catalyst to start the practical work, and so the Community Development Foundation (CDF) helped with the project design. The design is threefold, with an arts element, peer interviewing and outreach, the latter being the real 'meat' of the project. The Amber Valley Partnership funded the work, with substantial funding from the health authority, plus further funding from Amber Valley Borough Council and the Community Health Services NHS Trust.

All the information collected through the three methods (arts, peer interview and outreach) is being analysed and collated by the Community Development Foundation. Their report[4] has two purposes: first, to say what local people feel about Somercotes, and what their concerns and health needs are; second, because this is a pilot project, to compare the arts, peer interview and outreach methods in terms of how they worked with local people, how people felt about them, and whether they should be continued.

There were six arts projects, representing a range of approaches. Some of the workers had previous community development experience, while others did not. The Community Development Foundation provided training, which allowed us to develop the projects simultaneously, helped us to collect information in the same way and ensured that everyone understood the process.

Each project looked at cultural, environmental, social and economic areas of interest with the groups, in different ways, some more structured than others.

The first project was done by Class 5 in the junior school, who used photography. The children did a lot of writing and talking, and took photographs. All the work was collected in a book and an exhibition.

Interestingly, the children did not seem to give their own views of what they needed, but rather the views of their parents. This has its pros and cons. More people became involved in the needs assessment, but not all the children's views were represented. For example, the children asked for an aerobics class, obviously something their mothers had suggested!

In the second project, members of a youth club helped to make a video. With this, we wanted to look at what Somercotes had, and not just what it did not have, as well as looking at solutions. So the young people looked at what the cultural, environmental, social and economic issues were for them, and proposed solutions. One conclusion was that there is not a lot for young people to do in Somercotes – anecdotally everyone knew this, but it has now been properly recorded.

One of the issues that came out was a preoccupation with sex, as well as issues around sex education, drugs, and drug education. Such topics are very sensitive, so it was decided that two videos be produced – one for the youth club and one for the wider public.

The next project was with women of all ages. We had originally planned for them to work in groups, but people did not feel confident to do this, so worked individually. One group of elderly people worked on a Spanish piece. They felt that the local landscape was grey and dull, and they talked about where they would like to be, about their ambitions and their dreams, and so we did armchair flamenco dancing. They were very keen. One of their solutions was to persuade their doctors to recommend that they have more of that sort of activity, because they felt so invigorated by the exercise – and that has happened.

Work with a local theatre group has been postponed until the end of the project, when we will have a public presentation. The group will use playback theatre, in which people tell their stories to actors who then act them out, to air some of the issues.

We gathered oral history, largely with elderly people, who did creative writing, painting, and collected photographs.

The final project was a textile banner, part of a larger series with Amber Valley Borough Council. This looks at the positive things in Somercotes and records things which are needed, such as a bank and a children's play area.

Each of the arts workers could write down additional information as they thought appropriate, alongside what was produced by participants in each project.

The value of the arts project is that we now have a staging post. Something has happened that can continue in the community. It also celebrates what Somercotes has, not just what it does not have.

The second data collection method was peer interview, i.e. local people chatting to local people. We had hoped to contact approximately 10 per cent of the population of Somercotes by this method.

Interviewers were recruited through publicity surrounding the programme's launch, through a newspaper produced by the Amber Valley Community Development Service, and through organisations such as Neighbourhood Watch schemes, truancy watch schemes, the Amber Valley primary care groups, mental health services, and the local fishing club.

Training was given to all the interviewers to ensure that everyone completely understood the programme, enabling research to be carried out efficiently and safely. The interviewers were involved in designing the questionnaires.

Peer interviewers were paid expenses during training and for each interview they carried out, at a rate that would not affect state benefits. All the information collected by the peer interviewers was sent to the CDF for evaluation.

The third data collection method was an outreach programme, in which staff or public representatives whose duties brought them into contact with the public were asked to gather the views of their patients, clients and constituents. This included health service staff, councillors, housing wardens and the clergy, with the intention of interviewing two per cent of the population of Somercotes, making about 100 interviews. The Community Health Services NHS Trust asked permission from clients or patients to record their views, problems, ideas and solutions during treatment sessions and/or visits.

Health service personnel who work in the community were involved, such as the learning disabilities team, occupational therapy, district nursing and health visiting, physiotherapy, dietetics and the diabetes unit. Schools were involved through school nursing, and one of the clinics was involved through the speech therapist and the health centre manager.

Training was given, and five disciplines helped to design the outreach recording form. There was no individual identification apart from age, gender and ethnic group. Three arts workers, parish and county councillors and a housing warden were also involved.

Comments that came up included the loss of shopping facilities, poor public transport, especially for those with young children at home all day and for the old, and no bank or cash dispenser. There were also concerns about the environment, particularly smell and noise from industry. The solution was felt to be tighter control by the council over noise pollution and smell. More obvious policing was suggested as a solution to burglaries.

All these comments and information have been fed to the CDF who will shortly be producing a report.

Bibliography
1. Department of Health (1999), Saving Lives – Our Healthier Nation
2. Amber Valley Borough Council (1999), Amber Valley Partnership Health Strategy: Towards a Healthier Amber Valley
3. Amber Valley Borough Council (1999), Second Annual Public Health Report
4. Community Development Foundation (1999), Draft Somercotes Needs Assessment Report

Health promotion – health inequalities: A review of health with a community perspective

Jo Stott
Health promotion specialist
Hull & East Riding Community Health NHS Trust

The recent government health strategy Saving Lives: Our Healthier Nation[1] has the twin goals of improving the health of the population and narrowing the 'health gap', i.e. improving the health of the worst-off in society.

The strategy acknowledges that poor health arises not only out of poor lifestyles – smoking, inactivity, etc. – but that it is also linked to social, economic and environmental factors. The strategy states that 'poverty, low wages and occupational stress, unemployment, poor housing, environmental pollution, poor education, limited access to transport and shops, crime and disorder and a lack of recreational facilities all have had an impact on people's health' (p.42).

The Acheson report, Independent Inquiry into Inequalities in Health[2] recommended action on poverty, housing, education, food, water, transport, pensions, childcare and smoking. Reducing income inequality and helping families with children were designated priorities.

In response to the challenge of tackling health inequalities, East Riding Health Authority commissioned the Health Promotion Service of Hull & East Riding Community Health NHS Trust to undertake a review of the range and types of health promotion interventions which are being undertaken in the 21 most deprived electoral wards. In addition the review was to gather a community perspective on health.

As a community health development worker I had worked in communities before where external researchers or consultants had conducted research. The community response was still fresh in my memory: 'Why do they always pay outsiders to say what we could have told you? We are the experts.' So it was decided to test out a methodology which used local skills.

The East Riding Health Authority area includes the city of Kingston upon Hull and the East Riding of Yorkshire. The electoral wards to be studied were defined by Townsend Z scores (1991 census), taking into account the reorganisation of electoral wards following the division of Humberside County Council into four unitary authorities in 1996.

A steering group with representation from voluntary and statutory bodies was convened in May 1999 to support the project. The aims of the review were:
- to summarise the health and socioeconomic profile of the most deprived wards in Kingston upon Hull and the East Riding of Yorkshire
- to gather data on community views and perceptions on health and health promotion
- to review the type and range of health promotion activity undertaken on a local basis in areas of identified deprivation.

METHODOLOGY

In recent years there has been an increasing recognition of the need to strengthen and develop community capacity if health inequalities are to be reduced[3, 4]. Activities which strengthen and build communities range from creating facilities for social interaction to enabling communities to work together to identify problems and solutions. Our methodology therefore emphasised building on existing skills and networks, and supporting community activity. Three sources of information were used to provide an overview of health promotion activity and lay perceptions of health and the determinants of health.

1. Health and socioeconomic profile

Information was gathered via the locally produced Social Atlas of Need and from public health sources, covering the standardised mortality ratio (SMR); birth and infant mortality; a population profile; an economic profile (Income Support and benefit claimants), and welfare provision (free school meals, types of households, child protection, long-term illness, etc).

2. Community views and perceptions of health and health promotion

A methodology was developed to build on skills already developed in the community. Local co-ordinators arranged research sessions within their community, using selective elements of participatory appraisal methodology.

Participatory appraisal is a method comprising three elements – research, education and collective action. It is a family of approaches and methods, which enables communities to share, develop and analyse their own knowledge and ideas. Co-ordinators and session workers were drawn from the Hull and East Riding Participatory Appraisal Network. This network has developed a pool of local people who have been trained in participatory appraisal methods, are familiar with the use of highly visual tools and techniques and are knowledgeable about the local community.

A report will be produced by the co-ordinators for each of the wards, reflecting community responses to four questions:
- What does being healthy mean to you?
- What affects your health (good and bad)?
- How has this community changed in the last five years?
- What do you think local people could do to improve health in this community? What could others do to improve health in this community?

Wherever possible the local co-ordinator was a local resident or community worker, or was from a community organisation. The co-ordinators contacted local people trained in participatory appraisal techniques to enlist their support. The research was carried out by these session workers in pairs. The workers approached local people wherever they could be contacted in the community, at local meeting places, shopping parades or in schools and youth centres. The information gathered has been given voluntarily and anonymously.

The research was conducted between November 1999 and January 2000. Ten hours of research was undertaken in each area and the resulting information was then written up by each co-ordinator to produce a description of the local community and the responses received. The aim was to produce a research report that reflects a degree of local participation and a sense of ownership. It would provide a sample of local views, while also recognising and building on local community capacity for research.

A fee for co-ordination of the community appraisal and the session work was paid either to the individuals or to their community organisation. In some instances this provided an opportunity to earn extra funding for an under-resourced community organisation.

The community appraisals have been carried out with a community development philosophy, building on skills within the community developed by the Hull East Riding Participatory Appraisal Network, contributing to the community economy and infrastructure. Over 2000 people have taken part in this process.

The resultant reports provide a varied and vivid picture of life in these communities. Many responses reflect local and current issues at the time of interview.

Participatory appraisal is increasingly used both as a research strategy and as an educational process, particularly in the Hull & East Riding area. There will continue to be debates about power relationships between researchers and respondents and the importance of the qualities, skills and attitudes required from practitioners[5]. This exercise has provided an opportunity to test a method which involves local people as researchers, leaving as much control as possible to those who have been appointed co-ordinators. There is no doubt this will give rise to a debate about validity, reliability and generalisability, and lessons will be learnt from the methodology to inform future practice.

3. Overview of health promotion interventions

A questionnaire was found to be the most appropriate method of obtaining data on the range and type of health promotion interventions undertaken on a local (ward) basis. A very broad mailing list was compiled for each ward, from records and available mailing lists targeting any organisation which may conceivably carry out health promotion. Many of these may not perceive themselves as health promoters.

The results will provide information on:
- geographical focus and demographics of health promotion activity
- themes, topics and issues being addressed
- project management, including evaluation
- funding.

REVIEW FINDINGS

The community reports and questionnaire results are currently being analysed to identify common issues, to inform future practice and interventions. The resultant report will provide recommendations for future health promotion activity. In addition, a separate report will be produced for each electoral ward, containing raw research information for the use of organisations within those communities, to complement other research activity.

The review has generated valuable information and will help to further develop local strategic and operational plans for 2000/01. In particular the information will be used for the East Riding Health Action Zone (Community Health Development Programme, Service Modernisation Programme and Partnership Development Programme), Healthy

Living Centre development, the Health Improvement Programme and related health promotion activity. The Health Promotion Service will use the generated information to shape the 2000/01 programme, reflecting the need to engage in a wider public health agenda.

CONCLUSION

A wealth of information has been gathered using this methodology. The community research has involved more than 30 residents, and opinions have been sought from approximately 2000 individuals. On first examination, the individual community reports show many similarities in perceptions of health and awareness of the social determinants of health, in particular the importance of community safety, social and economic environment and transport. At the same time local issues are reflected and will provide topics for further investigation. In some cases action is already being taken, without waiting for publication of the report.

There have been some unexpected outcomes from this process. For example, an opportunity to carry out an appraisal of three settled traveller sites in Hull; debate with local community organisations about research methods; at least three co-ordinators have entered employment during the project; and, most significantly, there has been an increased interest in using community skills in research.

Bibliography
1. Department of Health (1999), Saving Lives, Our Healthier Nation London
2. Acheson, Sir Donald (Chairman, 1998), Independent Inquiry into Inequalities in Health Report, Stationery Office, London
3. Benzeval M, Judge K, Whitehead M (1995), Tackling Inequalities in Health: An Agenda for Action, Kings Fund London
4. Department of Health, op cit
5. De Koning K and Martin M (1996), Participatory Research in Health: Issues and Experiences, Redwood, Trowbridge

Notes
The Hull & East Riding Participatory Appraisal Network is run by a steering group of organisations and institutions, and piloted the use of participatory appraisal in the area. The network exists principally to provide training and a point of contact for people who have been trained in PA, or for those who wish to consult the network about PA. For further information contact the Hull & East Riding Community Appraisal Network on 01482 616616, e-mail: pranet.comfocus@tinyonline.co.uk

Gamesley on the Go: Sustaining organisational and community capacity for health

Melanie Sirotkin, specialist in public health (inequalities and partnerships), West Pennine Health Authority

Walter Sutcliffe, chair, Gamesley Residents Association

WHY GAMESLEY?

Gamesley estate in North Derbyshire was built in the late 1960s to house people from Manchester. The estate, in a semi-rural area on the outskirts of the market town of Glossop, is home to approximately 4,000 people. Most people (80 per cent) live in council owned properties and less than half (40 per cent) have access to a car.

Gamesley has an underprivileged score double the North West average. Almost a third of the population (27 per cent) is aged below 14 and 40 per cent of households have dependent children. Lone parent households make up 10 per cent of the total and births to single mothers account for almost a third of all births; 21 per cent of births are to women aged below 20. The population experiences poor health and early deaths from circulatory and respiratory disease.

Gamesley Residents Association (GRA) is an active group, which has campaigned on many housing and health issues over the years. The GRA now has a busy office in a small parade of shops offering welfare rights advice, a job board, a local newsletter, a fresh food co-op and a range of other activities, including a regular summer festival. The GRA has also organised campaigns, including a successful battle to keep a GP practice on the estate. The GRA are partners with the education authority in bringing health-related projects to the estate, including first aid and food hygiene certificate courses and computer classes.

BUILDING BLOCKS

In 1996 the arrival of a new GP with an interest in community involvement, and local residents' involvement in recruiting a jointly funded local health facilitator were important milestones in building capacity in the local community and within statutory organisations.

The setting up of a Health Authority Integrated Purchasing Programme (HIPP) pilot site in Gamesley provided an ideal opportunity to unlock the potential for working in closer partnership. The HIPP was set up to allow collaboration between organisations providing health care, and to plan and commission services at a more local level. Tameside and Glossop Community Trust took the lead role in the Gamesley HIPP project. Partners in the HIPP had a commitment to tackling inequalities and developing the public health role, as well as a desire to see more people involved in decision-making.

The HIPP's 'whole systems' approach led to two workshops bringing together local residents, commissioners and providers of services. The GRA and other community members were active in developing and participating in these workshops. The first workshop looked at public health, while the second focused on priorities, which were agreed as sexual health of young people; coronary heart disease/lifestyle/well-being, unemployment and substance misuse.

The workshops helped forge a strong partnership between local people, service providers and commissioners, and out of them came Gamesley on the Go. Partners in this initiative are Cottage Lane GP practice, Derbyshire County Council, Geoffrey Alan Church, Gamesley Residents Association, Gamesley Community Partnership Board, Glossopdale Primary Care sub-group, High Peak Borough Council, Tameside and Glossop Community Trust and West Pennine Health Authority.

GIVING ORGANISATIONS FACES

The process has presented a number of challenges. It has been important to keep people motivated and convinced that there would be some action. Regular meetings have meant organisations are no longer 'faceless'. The GRA has developed a key role in bringing agencies together, and chairs regular forums that help ensure activity is co-ordinated and common goals realized. Short-term practical achievements have also helped, for instance the estate now has a health centre in redesigned shop premises, offering services to parents and children, and a range of classes has been offered on health and fitness, aerobics and looking good.

LOCAL PEOPLE IN THE DRIVING SEAT

Gamesley on the Go is working because the local community is in the driving seat. All relationships take time to develop, but working together on the HIPP project and developing a Healthy Living Centre bid for Gamesley has helped to generate trust between partners. Organisations have learnt to share data and information with local people and to trust in the process of working alongside communities and other organisations. Capacity is being built within organisations as well as within communities. Statutory organisations are still learning how to listen and how to speak without using jargon. The GRA has learnt to value its hands-on experience and has learnt that at times it is necessary to be assertive. Everyone involved has begun to understand that there are multiple perspectives and a range of problems and solutions. We are all beginning to see that partnership working shows results.

GAMESLEY ON THE GO

We now want to generate community capacity and promote positive health by:
- encouraging inclusion and involvement of young people
- increasing community influence in planning and managing local health and social care
- extending the skill base and health-related work opportunities
- developing people, health skills and opportunities.

To achieve our aims we plan to:
1. establish a Community Health Partnership Board that can influence and guide local health and social care decision-making
2. build a self-sustaining skill exchange and small community business network maintained through a local exchange trading system (LETS), and by increasing health-related training opportunities
3. set up an electronic link providing access to health information and to local and external health services, facilities and opportunities and by extending the existing PCG sub-group Intranet to other places in Gamesley
4. create a network of peer educators trained to offer drugs advice, sexual health advice and support to young people
5. expand the 'exercise on prescription' scheme to include sport and walking.

We want to build on current activity and enthusiasm, promote inclusion and involvement in the life of the estate from all sections of the community and promote the breaking down of barriers within and between communities. Our intention is to strengthen and consolidate current community capacity through focused development of facilities and organisations. The lessons learnt from the project will be used to develop new ways of working within Glossopdale.

Gamesley has a wealth of local capacity and commitment. Partnerships between the Gamesley community and statutory and voluntary agencies are well developed and there is a commitment from all partners to continue the process of building both community and organisational capacity to better meet expressed local need.

PART FOUR

Communities and democracy

Community, democracy and health

Christopher Gates
President, National Civic League, USA

Let me begin with some history about the National Civic League. We were founded in Philadelphia on January 25, 1894, by a group of young civic reformers who all went on to achieve great things in their careers – the sign-in sheet for our founding meeting includes Teddy Roosevelt, Louis Brandeis (who went on to become a Supreme Court Justice) and Marshall Field (who went on to make a lot of money in department stores).

They were organising to take on the political leadership of America's cities, which were considered very corrupt in the late 1800s. The cities were run by political bosses and political machines, and those who were lucky enough to be on the right side of the boss and the machine received a lot of city services, maybe even a job, but those on the wrong side of that machine received none of those things.

Roosevelt and his compatriots were convinced that democracy should not and could not work that way, and so the creation of the National Civic League in 1894 led to the reform movement and the progressive movement in American politics, which reshaped how politics, government and governance worked in the US.

It might be thought curious that an organisation founded around this notion of democracy was chosen by our federal government in 1988 to run the United States Healthy Communities initiative. In 1988 the US Public Health Service sent out a request; they said there was something going on in Europe called Healthy Cities, and they were looking for an organisation that could take the best lessons from Europe through the World Health Organisation (WHO) experience and bring that model to the United States. Public health organisations, medical schools and health organisations said they would like to be the ones to bring that model to the US, but as we read the material and some of the original writing about this movement by people like Leonard Duhl and Trevor Hancock, it occurred to us that this movement was not about the provision of sick care, but something different altogether. So we said to the federal government that we did not know anything about healthcare as it is traditionally defined – sick care – but we did know a lot about community and democracy, and we were very interested in this model. The federal government, to the consternation of many traditional health organisations in the US, chose the National Civic League to bring that model to the United States.

And for the last 11 years we have been trying to encourage people to organise at the local level, because our sense is that we create health by creating community. If we can connect quality-of-life outcomes to the level of democracy in a city, a town or a neighbourhood, in effect we improve people's quality of life by connecting them to each other. Something that started out almost trying to emulate a European experience has become a fully fledged movement in the United States.

There is now an incredible amount of activity, as hundreds of communities organise themselves around the rubric of Healthy Communities (we refer to it as Healthy Communities; 'cities' is a loaded term in the US). In some cases those projects take on traditional health-related issues, but in most cases they do not. Instead, they take on issues like job training, education, community building, creating neighbourhood organisations – very non-traditional approaches to health.

In this movement we see people choosing to take control of the lives of their communities, which in some ways is different than the model we have seen in other places. In some parts of the world the Healthy Communities movement has been about people organising to get government to do either different things or more things; in the United States it is almost moving in the opposite direction. There is recognition in the US that the role of government is evolving, and that if we are to improve quality of life at the local level then government clearly has a role to play, but it will not be the government's job or responsibility to provide communities with their quality of life. Communities have figured out that they will take on those challenges themselves and provide their own quality of life.

Five or six years ago, as more and more communities started to move down this path, the healthcare providers said, 'This is really interesting, this talks about health in a positive way, it reframes health as a participatory process,' and they tried to grab hold of the Healthy Communities movement. For the healthcare providers who latched on to it, Healthy Communities is a framework for public relations, a way to explain their relationship to the communities, and some big healthcare providers have built neighbourhood-based clinics and provided preventative care at the local level, instead of in big hospitals downtown.

But our sense is that this is not where this movement will go in the future, and that healthcare providers – while they will be important players – cannot and should not control this movement. There is a real fight about that in the US at the local level.

There have been hundreds of success stories in the US Healthy Communities movement, and there are four keys to those successes. First, those of us who believe in Healthy Communities as a community organising movement firmly believe that for this movement to be a success we have to find ways to spend less money on sick care, not spend the same amount of money differently. This notion puts us in conflict with the healthcare providers, who contend that the Healthy Communities movement can be about spending the same amount of money. In the United States the spend on sick care is now creeping up to nearly 16 per cent of our gross domestic product, which means that, if the United States is probably the best country in the world to get sick in, it is probably not the best country in the world to stay healthy in. Healthy Communities has to be a movement about taking money from the sick care industry and spending it on job training, education, violence prevention and cultural facilities at the local level. It has to be about a transfer of resources.

The second is that the focus has to be local. This will only ever be a national movement in the sense that we will connect people who are active at the local level all across the country, but we doubt that this will ever be something that the federal government owns and creates as a national agenda. Where Healthy Communities has been a success, it has been because people have banded together at their block level or their neighbourhood level and have created a form of social compact with each other, shaken each other's hand and said, 'We are going to look out for each other, we are going to improve each other's quality of life'.

Another key to success is the notion of inclusion; for this model to work everybody has to be at the table, which is easier said than done in most American communities. It is easy to adopt the rhetoric of inclusion and involvement, but it is hard to do community organising and involve everybody, including those who have traditionally not been involved, such as women, people of colour and poor people.

Finally, Healthy Communities has to be about how our democracy works, about people finding new ways to organise, to identify what their issues are and how they are going to take them on.

In the US there is currently a big debate about the state of our democracy. People are convinced that we are in trouble. It is very apt that 105 years ago, when the National Civic League was formed, our democracy was in crisis, and it led to the creation of the reform movement and the progressive movement, which changed the face of politics and government in the US. We would contend that 105 years later, our democracy is once again in crisis, and that one of the movements that can lead us out of this crisis is the Healthy Communities movement, because this movement is about reinventing democracy at the local level.

Some of the reasons why US democracy is in crisis will also apply in the UK. One is that citizens find themselves incredibly angry. In the US politicians say that citizens are not engaged in civic processes because they are apathetic. But the definition of the word 'apathy' is that people do not care about their community, their country, their democracy. We do community organising all over the United States and we have to look real hard to find people who do not care. We find that people care very passionately about their community and about their democracy. They are angry about how politics works, they do not think their voice is heard, they do not think small people matter in the process, and so they choose in a very rational way not to participate in the process.

That lack of participation is the subject of a great deal of conversation in the United States. In traditional politics, politics with a capital 'P', citizens have deserted the political process. In the last congressional mid-term elections, 36 per cent of those eligible voted, a historic low. People also appear to have deserted the small 'p' politics of community involvement and community engagement.

Here we can mention social capital. Bob Putnam, a political scientist at Harvard University, wrote a famous article a few years ago called 'Bowling Alone'[1], in which bowling became his metaphor for the disengagement of citizens from each other. He cited the statistic that more people in the United States went out to bowl, but fewer people were bowling in leagues – we were now a nation of people bowling alone. He has uncovered data to indicate that we no longer have associations with each other, our families do not even eat meals together, we no longer invite friends over for dinner – we are slowly but surely disengaging from each other. We attribute this to citizens being angry about the broad societal process, and it is part of the goal of the Healthy Communities movement in the United States to find ways to re-engage these people and pull them back into the process.

The second reason is that the media in the US has become very ruthless. Those of us who are saying to people that if we just organise we can change anything, that we all have to work together and there is nothing we cannot do, have to battle every day against the media's drumbeat of cynicism, sarcasm and negativism. The media have decided that it is their job to tear people and institutions down. As a newspaper editor told me, it is not news when the bridge does not fall down, so when we want them to write stories about the great things that people do to pull together and to make things happen in a positive way, that is not news. But when citizens attack each other, when people say negative things about each other, when bad things happen in communities, that gets press.

For example, by any measure crime is down in the United States. Our neighbourhoods are now safer, we have less crime overall, and significantly less violent crime, even in urban areas and the toughest areas of the United States. Yet when any survey asks citizens what they think is the biggest problem in their community, they say crime – because crime is disproportionately covered by the media. Even as crime statistics have gone down, the coverage of crime has gone up, as we discover from content analysis of newspapers and television news. The public perception is that they live in unbelievably violent neighbourhoods, which makes it hard for us to do business.

The next thing that puts our democracy in crisis is the presumption of bad intent, a new notion about leadership in the United States. In the old days it used to be that we really wanted people to lead and were eager for people to step up and lead in their communities. And because we presumed good intent on the part of our leaders, it was easy to get people to step up. But we have now become very cynical about the notion of leadership, so that when people step up to lead we presume bad intent on their part, we presume that they are doing it to either help themselves or their friends, or to get rich, or all of those things. This makes it nearly impossible to convince average citizens to step up, get involved and play a role in their communities.

The last thing is that we now recognise that traditional politics – the whole notion of social change occurring through elections and actions of government – is broken in the United States, it does not work any more. People now view government as the defender of the status quo. Recent focus group research for the Kettering Foundation[2] found that the public did not see any difference between Democrats and Republicans, their notion was that the real difference was between people who were in power and people who were not in power; secondly, the public views the media in the US as co-conspirators with both political parties, and they are all in a conspiracy to not inform or engage citizens.

So we might say that citizens are bad people for not participating in their communities, and not participating in politics, but on a rational basis there are good reasons why people have dropped out of the political process and have been reluctant to become engaged in their communities. The Healthy Communities movement has tried to organise in the face of that cynicism and anger.

Communities in the US are currently debating theories of democracy, whether they recognise it or not. At one end of the spectrum is the theory of representative democracy, and at the other end is the theory of direct democracy. Representative democracy says it is government's job to provide public goods, public services, and that the government owns the public agenda. That may work at the state level and national level, but it seems that we do not believe in representative democracy at the local level, because the lesson that we are teaching citizens is that their only obligation to their community is to vote once every two years, which promotes disengagement of citizens from the quality of life in their neighbourhoods.

As people in the US have become more cynical about representative democracy, there is now a movement to go to the opposite end of the spectrum, to 'direct democracy'. This is a movement fuelled by two engines: cynicism about the political process, and the changing uses of communication technology. It is now possible to vote by phone; most local government meetings are covered live on cable television, and many communities have boxes that are attached to the television which they can use, in essence, to vote on what they are seeing or hearing. In the US the joke is that everything, both good and bad, starts in California; we are pretty happy with sushi, but recently a lower court ruled that the click of a computer mouse, on an e-mail or on the Internet, was the equivalent of a signature and made it a binding agreement. That ruling, if it stands on appeal, will change the face of democracy, and we will now circulate petitions over the Internet, and vote on the Internet; and if people can vote on the Internet, there is no reason why elections should take place on the first Tuesday in November every other year, when every Tuesday of every week could be election day.

Angry citizens are now saying, in this model of direct democracy, that elected officials are unnecessary intermediaries between them and the services they want from government. The local government can present their budget not to the city council but to me, live on television, and I can vote on whether or not I approve that budget.

Yet our experience tells us that that model also will not work, because it reduces democracy to the binary world of 0 or 1, and what makes democracy work is the notion of public deliberation. Public deliberation is the moment when I can make an argument with such force or such emotion in my voice that I can convince you to change your mind, it is the moment at which we can look in someone's eye to sense how strongly they feel about a subject.

Instead of representative democracy and direct democracy, a middle model is now emerging from the Healthy Communities movement – what some people call participatory democracy or citizen democracy. It is a model where government, business and non-profit organisations all work together with the individual citizens of the community to solve problems.

We have grown beyond the notion of government being the sole owner of the public agenda; now we are even going beyond the notion of public-private sector partnerships invented in the 1960s when banks figured out that when things were going well in the community, the bank tended to do better, and when things were not going well in the community, and there was lots of crime, and bad schools, and people were not happy, the bank did not do as well. Nowadays this model does not work, when local businesses have been sold to or replaced by national and international companies, and it becomes harder to convince the private sector to be engaged in local affairs. Corporations increasingly work by dropping somebody into the community, leaving them there for six months and then switching them to another community, so there is almost no local business leadership left any more.

The third partner at the Healthy Communities table is now the non-profit sector, sitting there as a full partner, and being taken seriously as leaders. But even if you involve the public sector, the private sector and the non-profit sector, can you get things done in that cynical, 'politics is broken' environment? No. We have to reach beyond institutions to talk to real people. Here traditional political science teaches us all the wrong things, it says that all political activism can be explained through self-interest, and that every activity is either people banding together to make something happen that will help them, or to stop something happening that will hurt them. But this theory tells us that we never have to deal with people, we have only to deal with institutions: neighbourhood organisations, not people in neighbourhoods; small business associations, not small business people. Our sense is that there is a whole new group of activists in our communities that are not 'joiners'; we cannot pretend that we have dealt with them by dealing with somebody else – a growing number of citizens who are so distrustful that they say 'Unless my voice is heard, unless I get a chance, unless I am involved, the process is illegitimate and does not count.'

For this model of citizen democracy to work, where government, business, non-profits and citizens come together, there has to be what is called civic space or safe space. Government has a hard time convening this coalition, because people do not necessarily trust them. So the provider of the civic space or safe space has been the Healthy Communities movement, broad-based coalitions that enable people to come together to say these are my concerns, my desires and my aspirations for my community, and this is what I am willing to do.

The Healthy Communities movement has become the vehicle through which citizens are reinventing their democracy, and this middle model takes the best of both ends of the spectrum, because some level of representative democracy has to continue, we need government, some entity to speak on all of our behalf. We need somebody to take on the public tasks of putting out fires, providing police protection and picking up trash, but we also recognise that citizens want to have their voice heard and they want to be more involved.

When we think about where democracy is headed in the future, our sense is that in the US we will have a mixed model; at some level we will choose to use representative democracy; there are other issues that are so important, so contentious and so difficult to deal with that we are not far away from having national referenda, where the entire nation could go and indicate their preference on a particular issue, using the model of direct democracy; a third set of issues will be decided through citizen democracy (participatory democracy), where we all collectively choose to take things on, and the fourth model will be areas where citizens say that they do not need government to do that for them any more.

An example of the fourth approach, direct action, is the Neighbourhood Watch movement, where instead of paying high taxes to have a policeman on every corner, we look out for each other. That is community, deciding to do more things ourselves.

It is controversial because some people view that as giving up on government's role. But our sense is that in reinventing democracy we are also reinventing what we mean by citizenship. In the US we are now coming out of an era which started in the 1940s, with Franklin Delano Roosevelt, where government was the predominant societal problem-solver, and we have gone through 40 or 50 years of people being very passive citizens. Now the era of big government is over, and Democrats and Republicans alike agree that government has to play a less dominant role — and that means that we have to be willing to step up and fill that gap. In the Healthy Communities movement we are reinventing democracy, and reinventing citizenship in a more muscular, engaged way. We are redefining what it means to be a resident of a community. It is not enough to vote, people have to be involved. They have to speak up, they have to help, they have to be engaged; we are moving down this path toward people taking on more responsibility for themselves.

Let me finish by defining the 10 characteristics of healthy communities.

1. They recognise that times have changed, they do not cling to the old paradigm, people are willing to think in creative fresh ways. Healthy Communities projects never work in communities where people say, 'That will never work here'.

2. They understand that resources come from all three sectors, that government or business cannot do it alone.

3. They practise collaboration and recognise their interdependence, and they use collaborative problem solving and consensus-based decision making.

4. They honour diversity while focusing on shared values – this is a tough one, the yin and the yang of community these days. In Los Angeles we go into neighbourhoods where the African Americans sit in one place, the Korean Americans sit in another, the Hispanics sit here and the working class Anglos sit there, without talking to each other or looking at each other. The body language is closed, people are looking down, there is no eye contact, because they think they are in a room with their enemy, because they are diverse. Our facilitators do a 'getting to know you' exercise, in which we say, 'Just want to get a feel for who is in the room today. How many people here think that the biggest problem that this community faces is that the schools are simply too good? Anybody?' No hands are raised. 'How many people here, just out of curiosity, think that what this community really needs is some more litter? Anybody?' 'How many people think that the biggest problem is that we have too many parks in this community?' At that point they start to chuckle, they uncross their arms and start to look around the room to see if anybody else is raising their hand, and they realise that, as diverse as they may be in that room, there are no advocates for crime, for litter, traffic jams or bad schools; there is a shared value, called community. And the whole Healthy Communities framework has been a powerful tool to organise racially diverse communities.

5. Healthy communities recognise that power has been widely and thinly distributed. They recognise that the old world of a few power-brokers in a neighbourhood or a community does not hold any more and that they have to treat every resident of the community as if they have a certain amount of power.

6. They spend as much time on the 'how' of change as the 'what' of change. Healthy Communities practitioners are not afraid of process. It is easy to be cynical about process – all those meetings, all those facilitators – but process is the key that unlocks policy solutions at the neighbourhood level.

7. They recognise the value of dialogue and public deliberation, while retaining a focus on action. Healthy communities have found a way to balance a healthy amount of dialogue, ensuring that everybody gets their say, while recognising that the conversation must lead to action. That gives people faith in the Healthy Communities process – they feel that they are heard, and then they see things change in their community, they see their ideas put into practice.

8. Their citizens are deeply engaged in both the capital 'P' politics of party politics and campaigns, and the small 'p' politics of volunteerism and philanthropy. They understand that social change has two avenues; one through the formal governmental process and the other through people and organisations choosing to do business in a different way.

9. They accept local responsibility, they focus on their community, not on Washington DC. They do not say things would be better 'if only the folks in the government would figure out what they need to do'. That is not to let the government off the hook, particularly around funding, but it is to say that the initiative has to come from the local level, that if communities are waiting for somebody else to provide their solution, they will not be able to get where they want to go.

10. They focus on the issues of people, not just institutions. It is very easy in conversations about community problem solving to talk about the health of institutions, not the health of people – 'The hospital is not going to like that at all,', or 'That is not going to be good for the big employer'. You have to push that to the next level and talk about the health of people, and the impact that these issues have on individual people.

Our hope for the Healthy Communities movement in the United States is that it transforms the way people think about their democracy. We think we are well on that path, but the depth of the crisis cannot be underestimated. The jury is still out as to whether our democracy can be revitalised, but one of the leading hopes for the saving of that democracy is this Healthy Communities movement.

Bibliography
1. Putnam, RD (1991), 'Bowling Alone: America's Declining Social Capital', Journal of Democracy 6:1, Jan 1995, 65-78
2. The Harwood Group: Citizens and Politics: A View from Main Street America. Dayton, Ohio: The Kettering Foundation Press

What it feels like for us

Owen Gillicker
Kelly McElroy
Ann-Marie Pickup
Gerry Stone
Local area co-ordinators, Social Action Research Project, Salford

The Social Action Research Project is funded by the Health Education Authority. Its four local area co-ordinators were employed because they were already community activists in their areas, in preference to 'importing' community workers from elsewhere.

Owen Gillicker

I work in the Chapel Street area, which is the south side of the university and down towards the civic centre.

Why did I become a community activist? I grew up in Liverpool as a gay man, and when I left school in 1978 (a very political period in Liverpool's history) there was nothing in place that I needed, so I became a community activist. I started an unemployed group for gay people and the first youth group in the country for gay people. I did that for a few years voluntarily until I got a job as a welfare rights worker, having done a number of courses.

How do I feel about being a community activist? Sometimes I feel privileged; changing something, and changing something well, feels good, because one has actually done something.

I moved to Manchester about 15 years ago, I am involved in lots of community work: the Chapel Street regeneration, the Healthy Living Centre on Chapel Street, I am on the editorial committee of a free newspaper, I am involved in the Manley Park Credit Union, and various community and neighbourhood committees.

Sometimes I feel really uncertain about things, I do not know where the future will lead me. Other times I feel as if I am leaving the grass roots level, where I wanted to start from, because I have ended up as somebody who fills out grant application forms, and I have lost that face-to-face contact with the people I am trying to help.

We started the residents' association in the block where I lived because in October 1997 we were told that the block was to be painted, and it ended up as a total refurbishment, which meant that we had to live in really bad conditions for about two years. We had scaffolding all around us for about 18 months.

A couple of us started the residents' association and the council's housing department said we would be lucky if ten people were to turn up for the first meeting – about 85 per cent of the block turned up. Everybody was really furious about what was going on. Everything was being done without any consultation.

We formed a very strong group, and I became seen as some kind of a troubleshooter. For example, when one lift was being replaced and the second stopped working due to over-use, I would phone up and say my next-door neighbour could not leave the block, he was seven floors high and on two walking sticks, and if nobody phoned for him then he was effectively a prisoner in his own home. Things like that had the housing service see me as some kind of an ogre, until I started working for SARP. The SARP label has helped me in the community to gain the respect that I think is needed.

I am also involved in other types of community work of a more personal nature; as a gay man I am involved with HIV issues and so on.

Sometimes as a community activist I feel I am banging my head against a brick wall, what with all the red tape and bureaucracy, and sometimes I feel as if I have been invited to meetings just to make up the numbers, because the so-called professionals have not done their job properly. A perfect example of that is being invited to a meeting about doing something for the kids in the area during the summer holidays. This was two weeks before the holidays started, and there was the neighbourhood co-ordinator, a youth worker and me. I know nothing about youth work yet I was invited to that meeting, and I think that was just to make up the numbers.

Sometimes I do get a feeling of satisfaction, but sometimes the feeling is of total apathy and I feel like packing it all in.

The area where I live has become rather yuppified, because it is near to Manchester and near to the university, and the sense of community is now non-existent. I have lived there since the 1970s, when they had the first regeneration. The people who lived there in the Seventies will not touch this new regeneration because of the way they were treated in the Seventies, and it is up to people like me, who live in the area now, to see that the regeneration of Chapel Street works. If it does not work, if SARP money does not work in the area, it is the last chance for the area, and I feel I have to put all my energies into this.

Gerry Stone

I believe that times have changed and communities are ready to take control of their lives, but the authorities, the health authority and local government, are not equipped or prepared to do it just yet.

I agree with everything that Chris Gates has said. We have heard about people being imprisoned by other people's perceptions: how very true. We were at a meeting and one of the officers brought in food for us, and a council officer said, 'They don't eat fruit in Seedley!'

We need community development. We need communities to develop. Living in the kind of community that I live in definitely affects one's health, and it is not just about people getting very stressed. People do not value what we experience because it becomes the norm. We had just bought a brand new car, and obviously that is not the kind of thing people have where we live, and somebody lit firelighters under our car. That was at half-past twelve at night, it is tantamount to possible manslaughter, because in my area it can take an hour and a half to respond to a 999 call, for something that could equate to one's children being dead in their beds.

Ann-Marie Pickup

I have been doing what I suppose would be classed as community work for more than 20 years.

After I had my first two children I found myself at home, and I thought, 'This is not for me, I am bored.' I found other people in the area who thought the same, so I set up a mothers' club on Wednesday afternoons, and we would meet at each other's houses on a rota. The house would be a tip afterwards and we would have to clean up, but it was fine. We sat and discusssed news topics, child health, contraception, how to pay the bills. I suppose at that time I was building social capital and networking – buzz words of the moment – but I did not realise it.

After a while I returned to work, but I did not stop there. I joined the Parent Teachers Association at school and I did fund-raising events, and I joined the governing body and I am now chair of the governing body.

Other opportunities came along. The council wanted to form residents' groups in our area. I think they thought that because they gave us a carrot of £200 to set up, we would do as we were told. There were council houses that had had temporary bathrooms built on at the back, supposedly for 10 years, but they were still there 25 years later. To cut a long story short, we were successful in obtaining £4000 to get these bathrooms changed and to get other remedial work done to the properties that so desperately needed it.

I moved on from there and I joined the community committee. These committees were set up by the council and were attended by officers and councillors themselves to deal with problems in the area. At first I thought this was just a paper-pushing exercise, I would go to meetings and there would be stuff that had been discussed at different committees and was just there for our approval. But now we have moved on, we are consulted more, we are given a say in what goes on in the area.

To give an example, I had done a presentation at a partnership meeting the previous week about Lower Kersal and Charlestown, and about how we were expecting to apply for extra funding for our area under New Deal. I had said to the chief executive of Salford, John Willis, 'You do not know the area'. I had photographs, but looking at photographs is not knowing the area. Earlier this week he turned up at our community committee meeting and I was gobsmacked, I was really pleased he turned up. We knew that the community committees were to get extra funding to spend in their area, per head of population. Where I live in Salford we have Castle Irwell Students' Village, and I wanted to know if the head-count included the 1600 students from that neighbourhood. He said he did not think it did, so I asked if we could have an extra £1600, £1 per head, and he said he did not see why not. That has given us an extra £1600 to spend in our area. It may sound a little cheeky, and as if we are always nobbling for money, but we are not.

There have been lots of burning issues in the area, burning probably being the operative word. Somebody decided in their infinite grace to set fire to the library. The library was built 50 years ago as a temporary building, nearly all of wood with a tarmac roof. We now have a new library, albeit another temporary building, and it is brilliant. We have got something back in place as a community focus, it is used by the children in all three primary schools and also by the older people in the area. That was about getting people together. I did not have to do it, they got up petitions themselves, they made representations to the council, people networked with each other. They realised that the social capital that they had, had got to be built on and things had got to be done.

Kelly McElroy

I have not done as much as Gerry, Ann-Marie or Owen, I have only been in community work for a year. I started voluntarily, I was unemployed, I was doing nowt and I started going into the local job shop and looking for work. A woman called Kim Addison managed to persuade me that it would be a good thing if I got involved in various arts projects, so I was working voluntarily with children and artists. A staff post came up, I was encouraged to go for it, I took it, and it has opened my eyes a lot to what is going on in the world. I did not know it was all about politics, but obviously it is.

Since then I have been focusing on the youth in my area. We have got nothing whatsoever. We have a resource centre, and a job shop, and that is about it. We have constituted a young women's group, we are trying to get a young women's centre open, and doing a lot more with the youth.

A lady from Salford Health Authority heard these things being said about people working in the community: 'Are they experienced enough?' and 'Are they professional enough to do something?' I think we are, and I think local people should be given the chance to speak out for their areas, and I am happy to have one of these SARP posts, as I know my colleagues are, so we can have our voices heard and somebody will take note.

PART FIVE

Identifying and mobilising community skills and assets

Social Action Research Project

The first section of this paper explains the project's aims, objectives, and background, and describes work undertaken in Nottingham. The second section describes work undertaken in Salford.

Nottingham

Dara Coppel
Public health researcher and evaluation manager, Nottingham Health Authority

Dr Nicola James
Lecturer in public health, University of Nottingham

INTRODUCTION

The aims of the Social Action Research Project (SARP) are to tackle health and social inequalities. Its objectives are to assess the notion of social capital and its links to health, and to build capacity for partnerships and for participation, to develop sustainable means of promoting health.

Social capital can mean different things to different people, so it is important to explain which definition is being used. The political scientist Putnam was one of the first to introduce the idea of social capital, and he defined it as 'features of social life, networks, norms and trust, that enable participants to act together more effectively to pursue shared objectives ...'[1]

In outline, the main elements of social capital are social cohesion, social relationships, social support, formal and informal networks, trust as opposed to fear, reciprocity, i.e. wanting to do something for somebody, or somebody else doing something for you, community and civic engagement and citizen power.

SARP IN NOTTINGHAM

The objectives in Nottingham are in line with the former Health Education Authority's (HEA's) aims and objectives for the Social Action Research Project as a whole. We want to provide baseline data on the levels of social capital in key areas in Nottingham. We also want to demonstrate the allocation of resources to community-based programmes. We want to involve communities in the planning, management and evaluation of initiatives, although so far we have not been able to do that as much as we would have liked.

We want to develop multi-sectoral working. Nottingham has some great partnerships and Nottingham city council and the Nottingham health authority are the two main partnerships in the SARP; other key players include local people, the Health Action Zone, the police, Nottingham University, the Greater Nottingham Partnership, local voluntary groups and organisations.

Our final objective is to set up a city-wide mechanism for developing social inclusion and tackling health inequalities. We want to work with other people who are involved in similar initiatives, and share with each other what we have learnt.

A baseline research project was part of phase 1, (the first of three years). Another initiative in the first phase involved local people who could have been socially excluded in developing and designing technology and information, using focus groups.[2] One of these groups brought together carers to talk about how they could use technology to feel more connected, what they would like to see in that technology and where they would like to access the technology. Other groups were of long-term unemployed people and elderly people. The baseline research team used non-participant observation of the focus groups and face-to-face interviews with participants. These were very successful focus groups. One lady was asked where she would go to meet people, and where she thought she might access technology, and she told us she did not meet anybody because she did not have any friends. Others within the group then told her, 'You can be my friend'; we have kept in touch with people, and they now get together on a regular basis.

Our Vision and Learning group involves people from the locality teams, from formal structures, informal structures such as residents' groups and people who attended focus groups. Its purpose is to share learning: what is going well, what is difficult, how we can get around the barriers, allowing people from key initiatives around Nottingham to say, 'Yes, we also have that problem, we got around it this way.' It aims to be a forum for discussion, which we did not have under the earlier steering group structure with its meetings every six weeks. We want people to feel that they can talk about what they want, in an informal environment. For reasons of accountability we also have a project board, and a 'housekeeping' group, which has been called upon a few times in emergencies, when we needed to bring people together to bash something out, or to use the right channels.

THE SARP BASELINE SURVEY

The objectives of the baseline survey were to collect baseline data on social capital, to examine the links between social capital and health, and to inform the development of initiatives related to community resources. The survey has been undertaken by the University of Nottingham.

We have chosen four areas from which to collect baseline information. There are two distinct areas: the St Ann's and Manvers local authority wards, an inner city area, on the one hand, and Clifton West and Clifton East, on the outskirts of the city, on the other. Both areas come under the same Primary Care Group. Using Townsend's scores,[3] they are both classified as deprived or most deprived, and have similar health indicators. They are geographically separate; another difference is that St Ann's and Manvers are subject to a number of government regeneration initiatives, such as the New Deal for Communities, Single Regeneration Budget, employment zone and others, while Clifton East and Clifton West have not been the focus of such initiatives, although they are classified as deprived areas. Both areas are similar in population size, and age and sex breakdown.

THE QUESTIONNAIRE

A questionnaire[4] was developed jointly by the SARP in Salford, the HEA and ourselves. Some questions are common to Salford and Nottingham, for comparative purposes, while others are local questions relevant only to our own areas. For the local questions we consulted widely to find out what people in Nottingham thought social capital meant and what they wanted to find out. The questionnaire was then piloted and amended before it was administered in face-to-face interviews in people's homes, taking an average of 45 minutes to complete. There were 116 questions, some of them open questions but most of them closed questions, covering demographics and their perceived health status. We also asked questions related to social capital; the main headings were 'Participation in local community activities', 'Reciprocity', 'Feelings of trust and safety', 'Connections', 'Citizen power' and 'Perceptions of (their) community'.

Instead of asking people what they thought of St Ann's and whether they felt a part of it, we asked people to identify the area they lived in, to define what they meant by their community. Some said it was their street, some said it was their neighbourhood and community, while others identified just a few key houses around them.

People enjoyed talking about their community but they did not enjoy talking about their employment and income, so we kept those questions until the end of the questionnaire – but they needed to be asked. We also asked questions to identify social class.

We recruited and trained people from the survey areas to be interviewers, following previous action research in Nottingham, based on Freire's model of education and political liberation.[5] Such participative research also allows the interviewers to learn new skills and earn extra money. We ran adverts on local radio, we had numerous articles in local newspapers, a freephone number and an office manned from nine to five so that people could phone in and ask for more information or for application forms. We put up posters in local shops, libraries and health centres, we contacted local people, community organisations and forums. Forty-five people came forward, but with more time I suspect we would have had many more.

We recruited 31 interviewers, to do a certain number of interviews each week in people's homes over a three-month period. They had to attend a three-day training course, for which they were paid. Only one person dropped out between interview and training course.

On the course we explained the objectives of SARP, and looked at communications skills, personal safety (this was a major issue: police told interviewers how to look after themselves in people's homes, all interviewers were given ID badges and copies were given to the police along with contact numbers). We also covered legal and ethical issues, including confidentiality.

We went through the questionnaire question by question, gave everybody a chance to role-play administering the questionnaire, and tried to give as much encouragement and feedback as possible. The role-play worked well, giving them the confidence that they could administer this daunting questionnaire with its 116 questions. They also felt more confident to query some questions, and we were able to explain the importance of collecting information in a systematic way. The evaluation of the training was very positive, and no one dropped out at that stage.

We had the evaluation tool, the questionnaire and trained local interviewers, now we needed a sample of interviewees. We used the Nottingham health authority's EXETER system, a database of all the people who live in Nottingham health district who are registered with a GP, which includes 98 per cent of the population. This database also gave us access to some secondary health information by patient. We wanted five per cent of the populations aged 16 and over, randomly selected by age and sex. That five per cent was approximately 1000 people in each area, so we were looking to interview 2000 people across the two areas.

One of the downsides to using the health authority's EXETER system was that the Director of Public Health on behalf of the ethics committee said that we should ask people to formally opt into the study, rather than just sending them a letter saying we would like to interview them and an interviewer would be knocking on their doors. So we sent a letter explaining what the study was about, with a reply slip and stamped addressed envelope, with the incentive of a £5 Boots voucher for all completed interviews. However, to interview 1000 people we had to send out 12,000 letters. We sent out nearly 7000 letters to Area 1, St Ann's and Manvers, and had a 13 per cent response; another nine per cent were good enough to tell us they did not want to take part, and the remainder did not reply even after we had sent out reminder letters. In Area 2 we sent 5000 letters, and a slightly higher percentage of people responded.

Thirty interviewers worked over three months, and even if the project had stopped there, we have learnt a huge amount. The project team met the interviewers every week to discuss how they were getting on, to collect completed questionnaires and give out more contact names and addresses of people, and they all really loved doing the work. We sent evaluation sheets to the interviewers immediately after the training, midway through the three months and at the end. They were paid per interview, but when we asked them what they were getting out of it, there was very little mention of the money. It was all about how they enjoyed meeting new people. And this crowd of 30 interviewers who had not known each other were now acting as buddies with each other, and going out to interview together.

We met on Mondays at 9.30am at a community centre. I asked one of the interviewers why everyone was already there when I arrived, and she said that they all met up at nine o'clock so that they could chat about what they had done the week before; she told me she loved Monday mornings. It was lovely, she said, there was such a range of people to deal with, older people, young men etc.

Another interviewer told me she got a lot out of being an interviewer because it was really nice meeting so many new people. She would drive past people's houses and think about the people who lived there, and who she had spoken to. She had also learnt more about the area she lived in.

One interviewer telephoned me to say she gained so much strength from being an interviewer that she coped with some very difficult family circumstances a lot better; another lady recently told me it was so nice being an interviewer because she was not mum, not the wife, she was an interviewer.

Only four interviewers dropped out, two because of work commitments, one because they got a full-time job on the strength of the extra skills gained from doing the interviews, and one because of family priorities. Nobody left because they were not enjoying it, or because it was too difficult or they did not get enough support.

We had 967 completed interviews for Area 1 and 998 in Area 2. We are now analysing the data.[5]

We have sent out evaluation sheets to the interviewees to gather feedback about the interview process, their thoughts about the questions, how comfortable they felt with the interviewers, whether they felt more comfortable because it was a local person, and so on. We also plan to hold some focus groups and interviews with key informants, to supplement our information.

We will check the reliability of our interviewers' data by sending a trained researcher to re-interview a sample of the interviewees, to check for reliability across the different interviewers.

CONCLUSIONS

One of our difficulties has been the timescale of the project. We wanted the interviewers to be involved in the planning process and in writing the questions that were to be used in the questionnaires, but time did not allow. We are encouraging them to get involved in the Vision and Learning Group, to be able to feed into what initiatives will come out of this work over the next few years. We have also passed on their details to other organisations who want to use their interviewing skills.

Another issue was the recruitment of the interviewers. We were trying to reach people who perhaps were not given the opportunity to do this type of work, but we were unable to recruit some people because they were on benefits and it was more hassle than it was worth, they could not afford to lose benefit.

We have a long way to go, but have already learnt a huge amount.

Salford

Emma Rowbottom
Manager, Social Action Research Project, Salford

INTRODUCTION

Our project is based in East Salford, the inner city area of Salford. We have also conducted a baseline survey, although we contracted out the work to the Office for Public Management, which in retrospect was maybe a mistake, but we did not feel that we could do it in three months. The HEA will be able to compare the two approaches.

Some people seem to think that social capital is a dirty word because it is a buzz word, but I think it is quite a useful theory. It is what people have been thinking about and doing for years, but now it has a name.

In Salford our definition of social capital includes:
- local identity – those who do not identify with their area will not put any effort into doing anything about making it better, or keeping it as good as it is
- levels of help and support given and received, or reciprocity ('you scratch my back and I will scratch yours')
- levels of trust, which includes respect for oneself and for others – probably one of the major elements
- perceived levels of power over the things that influence the life of the community.

We are about building social capital. We do not really know if that is possible, it is a research project. Sometimes we can get so involved in action that we forget it is a research project, that we are about measuring this. The way we intend to go about building social capital is through community action, using local people.

I have friends who are community activists and it wound them up that they would go to meetings with people who were paid so much money, yet who knew no more than they did. It was just by the chance of where they were born, what school they went to or what colour they are, that they were not sat there with the 'professionals'. In a small way we are trying to change that. If we were to sit the four people we recruited (see 'What it feels like for us,' page 101) in a room with no badges, no titles, nothing, no one would guess. No one would know that they were aliens!

How did we get these wonderful people? Like Nottingham we realised we could not do this in the usual formal way. We did not even go to newspapers, we just went straight for the posters on the walls of the pubs, the shops, the churches, the places where we thought community activists would probably hang out and would probably do their networking. In one of the areas it proved quite difficult, and as time has gone on I am beginning to understand why: there are not many places to put the posters, which is sad.

I found the recruitment process slightly strange. I am from a local authority and community background, but recently I got a bee in my bonnet about being a manager and I went on a management course. So what I understand about recruitment has come straight from a book, and it does not really fit when we are trying to recruit local people who might not have been working for some time because they are far too busy doing community stuff. So initially we went for telephone interviews, shortlisted and then went to a formal interview to verify a few facts before we appointed.

Some of those who came forward were well-known community activists and we almost expected them to apply. Some of those we expected to apply did not – and then there was Kelly. We had decided that the recruitment panel was to reflect the people we wanted to recruit, so we found two of Salford's amazing community activists, wonderful women who agreed to be on the panel for a fee. They could see things that maybe we would have missed. When we said that a girl was coming in who was 19, they said, 'What is she going to know?' yet when Kelly walked out of that room they were asking if they could get her moved to live on their estate.

There are things we would probably change about the recruitment process. Telephone interviewing was perhaps a little dodgy because of accountability issues, in that only I heard those telephone conversations.

We use an approach called 'working the whole system'. It was formulated by the King's Fund, and has been taken on by Urban Partnerships: 'Complex issues like urban regeneration or under-achievement in schools are influenced by the actions of many people and organisations. They are beyond the ability of any one agency to fix. Working whole systems shifts the focus of attention from the parts to the whole and offers a set of practical working methods to influence the way the parts connect and behave towards each other ...'

That is not a top-down approach, nor a bottom-up approach, it is about what goes on in the middle, about how we interact, how we begin to make these partnerships work, how we get community people to sit in the same room as decision-makers and doers, and get them to relate to and trust each other to share the power and begin to move forward.

We all know of Single Regeneration Budget (SRB) projects that have gone wrong in the past. There are SRB projects starting now that are still going in that same direction. People know it is not working but they have not yet discovered 'working the whole system'. In Salford that is the main method we shall use to build social capital.

Salford SARP includes a number of partners. There is the woman who is instrumental in getting SRB money into the city and making sure that it is spent in the right way, there are people from mental health services, from the Community Health Trust, someone from social services, from the university, from the health authority and the Primary Care Group. We have also invited people from the Housing Action Zones.

THE STORY SO FAR

We have four workers who live in four areas. Gerry Stone lives in Seedley and Langworthy, made famous (if that is the right word) by Newsnight. Newsnight are covering the regeneration plans on a monthly basis, and can show quite a depressing side to it. There are a lot of good things going on in that area, in quite a short time a lot of community activity is starting to build up. Some of it is not quite what the council expected, for example a group calling themselves Growler; but it is community activism, which is what we want. The issues in that area are voids (empty houses), crime, kids hanging about on streets with nothing to do. Through various communication techniques Urban Partnerships have decided that power is the issue. As Gerry said (see page 102), a very small number of the children in the area have power, not even 20 of them; the council has power, and the residents have no power.

One forum in the area is called SALI, Seedley And Langworthy Initiative, and they are starting to take power. It is so easy with regeneration to be led along at someone else's pace. I have been looking at plans for the physical regeneration and it is Day One: this, Day Two: this and so on. By this time next week they will have built the houses whether the people like it or not! What they need to do is to sit back and say, 'What is it we really want?' and Urban Partnerships are beginning to facilitate that, with training not just for the residents, but for officials who work in that area as well.

In Kelly's area, Ordsall, youth issues have come out of discussions with her, for obvious reasons. Initially the problems that surfaced were probably to do with respect and self-respect, and the way that young people in that area are seen, and the way they therefore act. They are seen as a problem, they are seen as kids who are hanging about. The area is notorious, it has the reputation of being the crime capital of Salford, and we are not talking petty crime. It has major gangs. These children are damned. We have put them in a prison made of our perceptions, we have decided that no one would want to go and work in Ordsall, that no one can work in Ordsall without two staff, that no female youth workers will go to Ordsall, that there is no point giving them anything because they will wreck it. We are working on breaking down those perceptions.

Kelly uses arts work to start discussions, and through those discussions the police came out as really winding the kids up, and vice versa. Breaking down that perception will never be easy, but maybe with some of the methods that the whole systems approach brings we might to begin to tackle that.

The first thing that was suggested was some community theatre. It involved bringing in a community theatre group, interviewing some of the young people, interviewing the police, finding out different views and putting them into a piece of theatre. Which is all right if you are middle class and you can drive home at night. Kelly cannot, she has to live there. If we started to make it look as if she was working with the police, she would be ostracised. If they decide that you do not fit there any more, you must move – it is that kind of place. Kelly does not want that, she loves living there, she just wants to make it a better place to live. So we have had to rethink the theatre, and she has been quite brave in saying, 'Hang on a minute, that is not what I want at all'. I have now learnt that we have to give people the time to really think about things and to decide if that is right for them and for their community.

Ann-Marie lives in Lower Kersal and Charlestown, two areas that have been lumped together. Those areas are preparing for regeneration, possibly some of the £50 million New Deal money. That area is on the brink of decline, parts of the council estates in the area have gone, every week they seem to knock down another block. The terraced area still has life in it, there are still flowers, hanging baskets, not too much detritus in the back entries – the little things one spots which mean people still care about an area. There is another council estate that looks all right from the front, but it is getting grotty on the inside, and it needs rescuing before it becomes another Seedley and Langworthy, before half the population is up and gone. New Deal might be the answer – or it might just be a plaster with a wound festering underneath.

There is an amazing amount of social action in the area. We have done a community audit, and that area just has so much – church groups, elderly people's groups, family centres, you name it, it is there, and not all run by the council. So the 'whole systems' work in that area will be about bringing those groups together to give them a stronger voice, for a start. We may also do a Future Search.

Future Search starts with a small group of key people in the area, including people from the council, the health authority and community representatives. We will start with perhaps eight people, go up to perhaps 20 for a planning group, with the odd subgroup, and it will take four to five months to plan an event that we hope will involve at least 200 people.

All of these people from many different backgrounds, people working and living in the area, will be in the room, and they will talk about their shared past, what was good about their shared past, and how it used to work, and how things used to be planned, and how things used to be. They will then look at what kind of a shared future they want. This event is not about wish lists, about council delivery, it is much more about 'if we meet with you, we can do that'. Something like a young mothers group can spring up from such a meeting and it is so much more powerful than the council taking a year to appoint somebody to be a nursery worker, because people have done it for themselves, they have gained skills, they have gained confidence, and it is much more sustainable.

That is probably the area where we can see the future most clearly at the moment, because we are planning a specific event. So Ann-Marie is probably the co-ordinator with the fewest worries about what her job is about! With the others it is more fluid.

The area where we are really struggling is Chapel Street. There is a regeneration programme here, mainly about getting more business within the area, and trying to make it into a media and cultural area. We have the university and we are not far from Granada Studios, so there is good reason for it, but the residents feel that they have been left out, they feel that regeneration has not worked before, that a new set of people have moved into the area who are not the same, people who have built massive brick walls around themselves, who have money for security to keep the other people out, and there is a real social divide growing.

Other problems are the lack of community facilities. They are about to open a Healthy Living Centre, but it is at one end of the area and transport will be a problem. Yet it will be the only place where people can have civic space, have a meeting place.

When we did the community audit we could have put it on one page. It was done in minutes. Similarly, when we did the recruitment I had nowhere to stick up the posters. It seems the community has really drifted, people are fed up with having gone to meetings and thinking that people were listening to them when they were not. Or if they did listen, they listened for so long, did a little bit and then it was back to 'We can only clean once every eight weeks, it does not matter if it gets dirty, that is the rota'. And that is what makes people so fed up, that kind of fixed attitude.

In 'working whole systems', we begin by finding the burning issue, and we are struggling to find that in Chapel Street. We cannot talk about better facilities for children because many of the new people who have moved in do not have kids. When they do have kids they will be moving to Cheshire, off to the hills somewhere. A large gay male population is beginning to form in that area, and I cannot envisage them having childcare problems either.

We might have half a chance with crime, because that affects both sides of the brick wall – except the enclosed section beyond the brick wall thinks that it is 'them out there' that do it. But as Christopher Gates said, it is possible to get people who think they are enemies into a room and break that down. And we will do that.

We carried out a community audit in all four areas, we counted our blessings. I had not realised how different that was; we were not looking at what is so awful about these areas, we wanted to know what was good about them, and then how we could make things better.

At the moment the community audit is a list of activities, activists and places where community activity can take place. We want to take that one stage further. We want to know what kind of people are holding this together, their gender, their age, their personal habits. That will be more important than we initially thought it was. It was an add-on, but it has a lot of scope for tracking how things grow throughout the project. We can ask people if they feel healthier if they meet more people, find out if there are more male volunteers coming through and so on.

Finally, we are building a virtual community. I had this idea that computers ruin communities, that kids were not going out and playing football because they were sat on the Gameboy. I was firmly fixed in that opinion until I came across Communities Online, and they explained that in fact people talk to each other through computers, and not just to people who live next door, but to people in America, in Holland, wherever. So it is actually building networks.

Within Salford University we have a section called Gemisis 2000 (Government, Education, Medical, Industrial and Social Information Superhighway), and we have commissioned them to start a virtual community forum. It was a very top-down approach – I went to a meeting, they said how about this and I said 'Yes, go on then', without asking anyone from the community. So we now have the facility, what do the community want us to do with it?

We have a growing number of community groups in Salford, but they never get to talk to each other except through the council – the council fetch people together for a tenants' board meeting once a year. There is a newly formed community network, but it is hosted by social services, so, although it is great, it means that the agenda is always set by someone else. In contrast, I love the freedom that a virtual forum would give the community, because then nobody is setting the agenda. They decide.

Such a network raises the issue of access to computers. Not everyone has a computer, they are quite expensive. However, Lottery grants can fund a computer. And linked to this, we held a focus group of unemployed men in Ann-Marie's area, to talk about computers. They hated the idea of word-processing courses, they thought it was something too horrible to even think about. But when we started to talk about taking them to pieces and blowing them up, we could see the enthusiasm start to build. So they have the funding now to start a very small-scale computer recycling course, leading to a computer recycling business. Each time they make a new one, disregarding those that they have blown up, they can sell it on. And if they sell it for £100 and it has cost them £50, that means they can go out and buy another two. Their aim is to provide people in their area with computers, because people want computers, but they cannot afford them. Single mothers are very keen to get their kids on computers because they do not want them to be left behind the others kids in school.

Bibliography
1. Putnam R (1995), Making Democracy Work, Civic Traditions in Modern Italy, Princeton, University Press, New Jersey
2. SHM Productions Ltd, City Net, Building Social Capital for Health
3. Townsend P, Philmore P, and Beattie A (1998), Health and Deprivation: Inequality and the North, London, Crook Helm Ltd
4. Freire P (1972), Pedagogy of the Oppressed, Penguin; Freire P (1974), Education: The Practice of Freedom Writers and Readers Publishing Corporation; Freire P (1985), The Politics of Education: Culture, Power and Liberation, Macmillan
5. Health Education Authority (1999), The Baseline Questionnaires for SARP, Working Paper, London, Health Education Authority

Walsall's local committees

Dick Hackett
Principal local policies officer
Local Governance Unit, Walsall Metropolitan Borough Council

Walsall council has prided itself on its community involvement, with an array of residents', tenants' and community groups and forums across the borough. In April 1996 Walsall won Single Regeneration Budget (SRB) funding, under the rubric 'Empowering Local Communities'. This will bring in £14.6 million of government money over seven years, to seven areas of the borough.

From April 1996 facilitators worked in these seven areas to prepare for local committees. Following community consultation, each area was divided into constituencies or 'patches' of approximately 100 households. In November 1997, elections were held for each patch. All residents in each patch aged 16 or over were able to stand for election and vote. Young people as a right can elect two youth representatives on to each local committee.

Lead officers from within the council were identified to work with each local committee, and act as an interface between the committee and the council. Local response networks were developed, made up of council staff, to work with local committees and respond to their agendas.

In December 1997 the local committees held their first meetings, elected officers, developed constitutions and standing orders. The committees vary in size from 16 to 30 representatives. They are making decisions on SRB 2 projects, influencing council mainstream funding and have a key role in Best Value.[1]

THE 1997 ELECTIONS

Nominations for representatives on the first committees were invited in August and September 1997. All households in each 100-household patch were issued with a nomination form, and a registration form for 16-17-year-olds. All nominations were verified against the Electoral Register and required the nominee to be seconded by three people from the same patch. A total of 139 nominations were received for 111 of the 151 seats, leaving 40 seats vacant.

Twenty-seven patches were contested across the seven local committees. A democratic process of electing a patch representative was required to fill these contested seats. The resultant elections are believed to have been the first of their kind in the UK.

Each person who appeared on the Electoral Register, as well as newly registered 16-17-year-olds, was issued with a postal vote. Voting opened on 24 October 1997, with the patch electorate being offered the option to return their ballot paper by post, or at ballot boxes situated in the Neighbourhood Offices in their area. Voting closed on 7 November 1997, with all ballot boxes and postal votes stored in a secure location. Counts in the local areas were held on 12 November 1997 and the results were published in the local press on 14 November 1997.

The turnout, as measured by the number of ballot papers returned in the contested patches, was 27.6 per cent compared to a borough average, in the council elections of May 1996, of 30.9 per cent. But considering the high number of seats filled, and the turnout figures in contested patches, these first local committee elections were regarded as a qualified success.

EXTENDING LOCAL COMMITTEES TO 10 NEW NEIGHBOURHOODS

After the establishment of the first seven local committees, the council was keen to extend them to other areas.

Walsall had previously received City Challenge funding, which resulted in some community regeneration. In December 1998 three new committees were elected in the former City Challenge areas of Caldmore, Palfrey and Birchills, to maintain and strengthen community involvement in the Challenge areas, and as part of an exit strategy from City Challenge funding.

The council's successful SRB round 4 bid included the establishment of local committees in Blakenall, Leamore and in five neighbourhoods in the Darlaston area. Work with local people led to the setting up of five local committees in Blakenall, Dangerfield, Fallings Heath, Blockall and the Green and Rough Hay.

Interest in local committees has been wide, and residents in New Invention and Rushall expressed an interest in establishing local committees. The council agreed to support this, and following joint work with local residents and council officers, a further two local committees were established in these areas in December 1998.

By the end of December 1998, 17 local committees had been established, based on the model of democratically elected local residents, each representing approximately 100 households.

Two more local committees were due to be established in Leamore and Heathfield, with elections due in November 1999.

THE DECEMBER 1998 ELECTIONS

For these elections a system for telephone voting was developed between council officers and British Telecom, in addition to the postal ballot system previously used. It is believed that this was the first time in any type of democratic local government election that telephone voting had been used.

The ballot for both the postal and telephone voting opened at 8 am, Monday 23 November 1998 and closed at 5 pm on Friday 4 December 1998.

The telephone voting system enabled residents in contested patches in the Rushall local committee area to register their vote via any touch-tone telephone, in addition to a dedicated line provided by British Telecom in Rushall Neighbourhood Office. The system was developed so that residents whose first language was not English could choose one of six Asian language lines to receive information about the candidates and to cast their vote.

Particular attention was paid to ensuring confidentiality and security of votes cast. BT and Walsall council held separate databases. BT produced a list of 12-digit Secure Voter Identification Numbers (SVINs), which had been generated randomly. The council electronically allocated each eligible voter with a SVIN (by randomly matching SVINS to electoral registration numbers). BT did not have access to voters' personal information and likewise the council did not have access to who had voted and for whom. Data was transmitted between the two databases via encryption coding, and there was password protection on all files. The chances of someone guessing the 12-digit SVIN of another voter was 1 in 800 million (you are 50 times more likely to hit the jackpot on the National Lottery!).

The voting lines were open 24 hours a day, with a council-staffed helpline available during extended office hours, including weekends.

Counting of the telephone votes was instantaneous, with results available in less than an hour of the close of the ballot. Counts in the areas using the postal vote system took place on 9 December 1998, in local community venues.

The telephone trial was very successful in technical terms, but the percentage turnout was marginally lower than in the local government elections held previously in the year. Telephone voting can only give the electorate another opportunity to exercise their democratic right, regardless of disability or language, and Walsall council understands that people will only vote if they think there is something worth voting.

Overall, the electorate in the contested local committee elections in December 1998 totalled 11,386, with the total number of votes cast 4,370. But due to the use of multi-representative patches in the Rough Hay area a simple percentage turnout is not easily calculated. However, taking this into account and allowing that the electorate in that area voted for two representatives as required, a turnout of 33.28 per cent has been calculated. This figure, compared with the turnout in May 1998 in ward elections of 25 per cent, is very encouraging.

Further analysis also shows that in one of the contested local committee patches in the Palfrey area, a turnout in excess of 60 per cent was recorded, with many other areas recording turnout levels in excess of 40 per cent. The trends have mostly been positive, and negative trends in some areas were small in comparison.

It is pleasing to note that a high number of the ten 'new' local committees had all of their patches represented, and that the majority of the seven previously established local committees had increased their membership.

BEST VALUE AND LOCAL COMMITTEES

In 1998 Walsall became a Best Value pilot on the basis of area-based multi-functional contracts within the seven initial local committee areas.

Each of the local committees had been approached concerning their involvement in the council's Best Value submission. All of the local committees agreed to participate in this initial approach because it provided an opportunity to influence mainstream service provision, which is vital to ensure the long-term sustainability of the local committee process.

Local performance plans were developed in each area, with the help of Action Learning Sets – small groups of elected local committee members, council officers and representatives from partner agencies such as the health authority, police, Chamber of Commerce and educational establishments.

This approach is resulting in unique consultation with citizens because the democratically elected, local committee members are consulting directly with their constituents and feeding the outcomes into the service review process. We believe that much can be learnt from this work and we will continue to promote the council's approach to the delivery of high quality, cost effective services that deliver Best Value within a unique democratic process.

PARTNER INVOLVEMENT

Local committees have benefited from the interest and commitment of partner agencies who have recognised the value of doing business with legitimate, democratically elected committees of local residents. The health authority, police, Walsall College of Arts and Technology, Chamber of Commerce, Training and Enterprise Council and the Council for Voluntary Services have all signed up to the local committee concept as a way of making things happen in local communities.

Representatives from these partner agencies are often co-opted directly by the members on the local committees and contribute to the development of their programmes and decision-making. The agencies use local committees as 'sounding boards' for ideas they may have or indeed, more formally, when they are required to consult local committees. The health authority and the police in particular have both made extensive use of local committees.

Each of the agencies has identified 'link officers' to work with local committees. These officers act as the representative for that organisation and act as a conduit to ensure a holistic approach is taken and a rapid response is possible when required.

Walsall has Health Action Zone (HAZ) status and local committees underpin our Health Partnership's vision of improving the health of our residents through community engagement and regeneration. Extensive public consultation has taken place on the development of Walsall's HAZ themes and Health Improvement Programme. Mechanisms are being introduced for co-ordinating HAZ programmes and the identification, development and evaluation of local projects, at a local level, which involves a representative of each local committee working alongside relevant

Primary Care Group representatives, local agency workers and the voluntary sector.

Walsall's HAZ will be locally determined by local residents from local committees, who will seek local solutions to meet local needs. True partnership in action!

An ongoing development is the creation of teams of all the agency link workers for a group of local committees, which meet regularly to ensure 'joined-up thinking' and the development of 'joined-up working'.

The democratic transparency of local committee development and the continued support of relevant partner agencies will seek to ensure the sustainability of local committees.[2]

Bibliography

1. Best Value is a government initiative designed to promote better quality services at reasonable cost, and more say for local people. Local councils are required to review all their services over five years, set tough targets for improving them and publish a best value performance plan every year to show how they are doing.

2. More information about the development of local committees can be found in the Walsall Metropolitan Borough Council publication, 'A story to tell – neighbourhood governance in the borough of Walsall'.

PART SIX

The way ahead

Round-up and the North West Charter for Partnerships

Professor Jennie Popay
Director, Institute for Public Health Research and Policy, University of Salford

This round-up will highlight a number of themes that have run through the conference, and give a sense of the practical issues that people were debating in workshop discussions. Finally, I would like to introduce the idea of developing a charter.

Six themes have run through this conference:

1. The need for more openness and lateral thinking about our understanding of community and community development. In particular, an important point was made about not getting locked into seeing communities solely as local people living in particular places. 'Community' needs to be defined in a broad and open way.

2. There was some degree of consensus about the values underpinning this notion of community development. In lots of different ways people seemed to be talking about building and supporting the capacity of communities, variously defined, to act collectively in their shared interests. There is enormous diversity in how that might be done, and we do not need to worry about getting a consensus about how, but there is a consensus on the notion of why and the values that underpin it.

3. There has been a very strong focus on the need for a strategic approach. Historically community development in the UK, North America and in other parts of Europe has lacked this. Further discussion may be needed about what a strategic approach means. We have talked about the need for a framework for shaping and directing the millions of flowers that might bloom, not to control the flowers, but to set an environment in which to develop. We have the beginnings of that, for better or worse, in Our Healthy Nation.

4. The other strategic issue repeatedly highlighted is the importance of not just focusing on the capacity of local people living in poor areas, but on building the capacity of

organisations in different sectors, to value the contribution and resources of local communities. We must recognise the key, pivotal importance of organisational development in building the ability of policy makers and practitioners at all levels to recognise and value the diversity of knowledge and expertise. That is one of the critical barriers to community development.

5. Christopher Gates' presentation clarified the link between the public health agenda, community development and democratic renewal. There is a tendency to think about community development in the health field as doing something about health problems, rather than shifting the very basis of how we govern ourselves. Gareth Williams and I have talked about the lack of a public sphere for debate, discussion and resolution in the last 20 years in England,[1, 2] echoing what Christopher described as a safe or civic sphere.

6. During the conference many references have been made to the need to be explicit about the fact that we are talking about power and the redistribution of power. I tend to think that the North American agenda does not place the power issue in the foreground in the way that it traditionally has been in England, although it may be the language. But maybe we also need to think in a more sophisticated way about what we mean by power. In the group I was at, people questioned whether power equals money or resources, and whether people have power that they do not know they have, and it was argued that community development work aimed to enable people to understand what power they have.

I have been struck by how tremendously rich the discussion was in terms of practical things that can be done. Nationally the agenda these groups were talking about is tied into that now being set for the proposed Health Development Agency, the organisation that will supersede the Health Education Authority. One issue is the need to collate evidence of what works; another is about what works for who, paralleling the evidence-based healthcare movement. Lay people as well as professionals need access to that information, so an important step is collating and making available that kind of information to diverse audiences. Another suggestion was a database of good practice in community development.

At a national level, enabling legislation is important. Flexibility is part of the Health Action Zone agenda, although it is not yet clear how much scope for flexibility there will be. At a national level also there is a need to unlock more resources: this is linked partly to legislation, but it does not all need legislation. People have also argued for national action to push forward organisational development.

On this point, it is appropriate to mention here a collaboration between the King's Fund, Salford University's Institute for Public Health Research and Policy, and Liverpool University's Departments of Social Policy and Social Work and Public Health, on a project which illustrates how the government is beginning to address organisational development. We have been funded by the Department of Health to support pilot work attempting to build the capacity of public sector organisations to work more equally with local communities. The project has four parts: a literature review; pre-pilot work developing practical ideas to inform a series of pilot sites where different approaches to capacity building will be tried out; the pilot work itself, and a peer review evaluation[3].

The need for the NHS, the Regional Development Agency and the Regional Assembly to develop more joined-up planning and policy making was part of many group discussions. The critical importance of employment policies and economic development, again at a regional level, was also highlighted. This was felt to be pivotal given that one of the barriers identified by some of the local activists to the organisational and professional changes they wanted was the fear of job losses in the public sector, as tenants took control of their own housing, for example. People also pointed to the region as a location for redistribution of resources from the better-off to the less well-off.

At a local level there were lots of ideas about how to train managers to encourage them to see issues from the community's side, which would help them to better appreciate the rich resources communities have to offer.

Finally, there have been two very practical suggestions:
1. To develop a charter around sustainability, community development and partnership. Such things can be symbolically very important, for example during the 1980s an influential charter was developed in Leeds around public health.
2. To collate a registry of local initiatives relevant to community development in health. This will be pushed forward by the Health Development Agency.

Bibliography
1. J. Popay, G. Williams. 'Popular Epidemiology' In J. Gabe, D. Kelleher, G. Williams (Eds), Challenging Medicine, Routledge, 118-139,1994.
2. J. Popay, G. Williams, 'Public Health Research and Lay Knowledge', Social Science and Medicine, 1996, Vol. 42;5;759-768
3. More details of this work can be found on the project web-site www.kingsfund.org.uk/saphc

Going strategic locally

Professor John Ashton CBE
Regional director of public health/regional medical officer
NHS Executive North West

What would it mean if we were to go strategic on community development and community organisation? During this conference we have heard some of the history and some of the changes that have taken place in these approaches and in their sponsorship and ownership. We are only too aware of the current limitations in our capacity to develop them. So the issue is how to go strategic, particularly in relation to our new national public health strategy.

What would be the implications of going down this path? What would a health authority look like if it was functioning in a supportive way to community development as an approach, and as a major vehicle for making a difference? How would it be different itself? What would it be doing differently? And not only health authorities but also Primary Care Trusts as they develop; also acute trusts, mental health and community trusts. What would it mean? And what about local authorities and the other stakeholders and key players? If there was a shared understanding of what it means to be building social capital, building capacity in the community, developing real partnership between professionals, managers, the public, the private and voluntary sectors, what would it look like?

What would be the tools? What tools do we already have? Where do they come from and what are our blind spots? Why are we limited in the ways we think about these things? Why are we restricted to thinking about money and doctors and nurses and beds when we think about health? What are the tools for thinking differently and making things happen in different ways?

Do we perhaps now need directors of resources rather than directors of finance – professionals for whom money is but one, albeit important, resource for protecting and improving health? If we focus on finance we tend to think in terms of how many doctors and nurses and beds the money can buy, and hospitals, bricks and mortar. However if we think of resources, of people, of homes and neighbourhoods, of social networks, of skills and transport we can begin to mobilise a much greater pool of resources using the dedicated finance that comes down to healthcare budgets. And if we collaborate with other budget-holders we can mobilise even more resources. It is fundamentally about building and recognising capacity wherever it is, and mobilising people and communities. How do we get the bureaucracies thinking in that kind of way?

Running through all of this is the question of what would then be the implications for all our education and training establishments – for what they are doing at an undergraduate, postgraduate and continuing professional development level? For the whole range of people who have a part to play, not just those who are in personal health and social care, but the people involved in housing, recreation, transport and the police. Today I talked to the five chief constables of the North West. We are discussing together the development of a joint public health agenda for the region and we talked about community development in our discussions. What are the implications for the police of working differently and making sure we are joined up? And it doesn't stop there. Are our universities and colleges really a resource to their communities, or just a meal ticket for professionals? What about access and outreach, settlements and community-based practice units, adult education and open learning? It is a big but exciting agenda.

Within the litany of World Health Organisation documents, the 1986 Ottawa Charter on Health Promotion is of particular importance.[1] Symbolically it was important because it marked the point at which the inappropriate export of technical western models of healthcare to so-called developing countries was challenged in a very explicit way.

Since the end of the second world war the Europeans, Americans and Canadians had spent 20-plus years going to overseas countries telling them what they really needed was all-singing, all-dancing district general hospitals and professionally trained healthcare workers; that they should take no notice of the traditional midwives, healers and herbalists because they did not know what they were doing, were unhygienic and that kind of thing – no mention of the 30-40 per cent of western trained doctors and nurses with unsatisfactory hand-washing practices – that what they really needed was to have proper health professionals; and when they trained them and when they built the big hospitals they found the entire budget was spent on a teaching hospital in a capital city and there was nothing left for anything else. Furthermore they had undermined the traditional healthcare system, and the new professional healthcare workers who they had trained wanted to either stay in the capital city where their children could go to good schools and they could go to the theatre, or they wanted to emigrate to the more developed countries. This pattern is recognisable here too! So we had undermined the whole system and not replaced it with anything.

What came out of the disenchantment with this, beginning with the Alma Alta conference in 1977, were the community development approach and the emphasis on primary care in a public health context.[2] We have not talked much about primary care groups and trusts at this conference but the three functions of these are to improve the health of the local population, to provide good personal health and social care and to commission specialist care. Public involvement and partnership are essential for all three functions if they are to produce equitable health improvement.

I am sure that most people here will be familiar with Arnstein's ladder of citizen participation.[3]

Figure 1 **Arnstein's ladder of citizen participation**

It is old-hat stuff from the Sixties and comes from community architecture but it is still worth thinking about. In healthcare-related areas and in public health generally, we still tend to think we are doing quite well when we get about halfway up the ladder. The implications for really moving towards citizen control, in the way that Christopher Gates described and in the way that community delegates have discussed, will require major changes in the ways we think about the organisation and delivery of public services.

In his 1988 report, Public Health in England, Donald Acheson revived Winslow's 1920 definition of public health as 'the science and art of preventing disease, prolonging life and promoting health and efficiency through the organised efforts of society' (Fig. 2) [4, 5].

One of the things that bothers me about the way the new Health Action Zones are shaping up is that they tend to be redefined back into personal health and social care, and there is usually little environmental action. When we are thinking about community development and community organisation for health, and for investing in health, we have to think about the whole health system and the range of policies and programmes that impact on health, not just the healthcare system with its focus on personal health and social care – it is a big agenda.

(after Winslow)

Figure 2 Public health

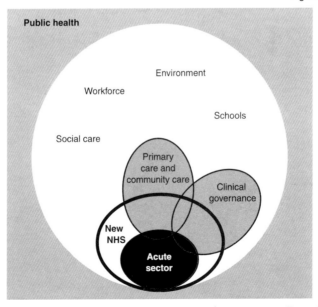

Figure 3 Health system

Here I would like to make a plea, as part of a personal crusade! Let us encourage people to talk about the health system when we mean the health system, and the healthcare system when we mean healthcare system. If we do that consistently it would be really helpful. I was at a meeting recently with some very senior people from WHO talking about the health system when they meant the healthcare system. It is unbelievably sloppy and it causes confusion. The health system is all the things we have been talking about at this conference; it is housing, employment, transport, agriculture and much besides. It is all the things that determine health (Fig. 3). The healthcare system is just a bit of the picture. It is a significant bit and it is not to be ignored, but it is only a bit of the picture. If we can get people to use the language consistently and clearly we might stand some chance of getting the various bureaucracies to develop policies that address these things.

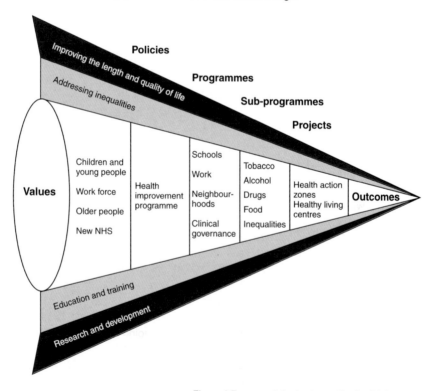

Figure 4 **Framework for implementing health improvement**

Figure 4 is an attempt to represent the whole national public health strategy in one diagram. It seeks to demonstrate how the values behind the government's policies are to be translated into action and improved health outcomes.[6] One could add the values from the Ottawa charter:

- building healthy public policies
- developing supportive environments
- strengthening communitis
- developing personal skills
- re-orientating health services.

In our discussions one or two people have been arguing that the national strategy has very biomedical targets. I do not apologise for this because these targets relate to causes of death and disability which amount to gross inequality – reducing such inequalities is what the strategy is about. What is important to consider is how we do this. It is through that set of policies, programmes, sub-programmes and projects illustrated in Figure 4 that these improved outcomes will be achieved.

If we think about all the sub-components of the strategy and view them through community development and community organisation eyes, we have to ask what it means if we are thinking about empowerment, community development and community organisation for children and young people, for the workforce, for healthy workplaces and for neighbourhoods. What does it mean for Health Improvement Plans and programmes? Will these plans be ex-cathedra and top-down, or will they be meaningful attempts to obtain community ownership by those communities and communities of interest affected by these Health Improvement Plans? How can we ensure that this happens?

It is the same with the specific programmes contained within the strategy as shown in Figure 4, and we could add to this teenage pregnancy and other initiatives as they come along. As Chris Gates has already mentioned, the political reality is that governments need quick fixes and early wins to maintain their voter credibility. The current administration is saying that it wants short-, medium- and long-term deliverables, which is unusual. The trick will be to explore ways in which that is possible by deploying a community-orientated approach.

One problem is that there is a great deal of good work going on at a grass-roots level and elsewhere, but it is not joined up. There is no infrastructure for these approaches, the work is rarely systematic or strategic and it does not achieve population coverage. To take the example of health-promoting schools, there are quite well worked-up theories about the whole school approach, particularly that which has been developed in conjunction with the World Health Organisation. Within the North West I am told that 12 of the 16 health authorities include boroughs that are doing some kind of 'whole schools' approach. But in terms of benchmarking what that means, we do not have a clue. If we were to look at the extent to which these health-promoting schools are really tapping into community asset mapping and capacity building, being a resource to their communities, from where would we start to get that picture? Unless we do that systematically and take a strategic overview, the danger is that we will contribute to a widening of the inequalities in health. Schools that are well put together in cohesive neighbourhoods or with well resourced families will move further ahead than others: it will be random and haphazard rather than systematic.

One of the recommendations of the Acheson report on inequalities in health was that in future all government policies should be assessed against the extent to which they reduce inequalities in health.[7] If we argue that we do not wish to take a strategic view, that we only want to get on with our own projects, we are colluding with potentially increasing inequalities in health. Somebody needs to be taking a strategic oversight of what is going on with particular reference to asset mapping, capacity building, developing and supporting community leadership.

I have at home a copy of the original Rathbone plan for community nursing in Liverpool in 1862. This map defines the neighbourhood-based districts which were the foundation for what became a national system of community nursing. There was a systematic approach to developing community nursing which made sense on the ground. We need again to be systematic about thinking through community organisation and development, and about the areas and groups that are involved. Paul Henderson has spoken of the need to avoid being hostage to the traditional idea of communities being all geographic. We must also consider communities of interest and a range of types of community.

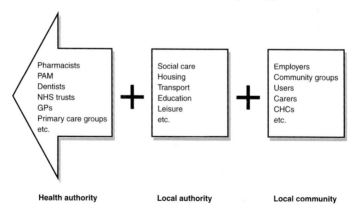

| Pharmacists PAM Dentists NHS trusts GPs Primary care groups etc. | + | Social care Housing Transport Education Leisure etc. | + | Employers Community groups Users Carers CHCs etc. |

| **Health authority** | **Local authority** | **Local community** |

Figure 5 Partnerships for health

The partnerships that need to be involved are very wide-ranging (Fig. 5). Chris Gates has made the point about direct democracy rather than representative democracy. Civil society is becoming complex, with mixed patterns of involvement and representation. The challenge is to secure the collaboration of multiple partners in a meaningful way and to identify which partner brings gifts to the party in improving the health of the community.

We shall need intelligence for that. One outcome of the national public health strategy will be a public health observatory in each region. We must ensure that these are not biomedical entities but that they connect to other types of intelligence for public health: social and environmental, but above all, lay knowledge.

One of the useful ideas in the public health strategy is contained in the grids for making explicit contracts for health (Fig. 6.) The notion is that in the process of health protection and improvement there are certain things which government must do, certain things which local agencies must do and certain things which individuals and families must do. We need to consider this grid from a community development perspective.

A National contract on:	Government & national players can:	Local palyers and communities can:	People can:
Social & economic			
Environmental			
Lifestyle			
Services			

Figure 6 Contracts for health improvement from Our Healthier Nation

One of the problems in this area of work, as in so much else in life, is of different community groups not getting on with each other, not being willing to learn from each other and being generally very 'turfist'. We suffer from the 'not invented here' syndrome – people who will not do something if someone else has done it first. I hope that by introducing perspectives from North America to this conference we have seen the benefit of being open to other people's ideas and experiences. We need to be much more open in this way locally and regionally, too. We need to be hungry and thirsty for best practice, to be willing to copy people with good ideas. There is nothing wrong with that. We need to create a culture that is willing to steal people's ideas if they are any good!

I have not answered the question I set myself at the beginning – about what it would mean if we adopted community development and organisation as a vehicle for delivering public health strategy. We need to think about that together. The challenge is how to get the public sector and other agencies up to speed; to be able to work functionally, effectively, properly and respectfully with communities.

Bibliography

1. World Health Organisation, Health and Welfare Canada, Canadian Public Health Association (1986) Ottawa Charter for Health Promotion. WHO, Copenhagen.

2. World Health Organisation (1978) Alma Ata 1977. Primary Health Care. WHO, UNICEF, Geneva.

3. Arnstein, S., (1969) A ladder of Public Participation. Journal of the American Institute of Planners. Quoted in Wates, N., and Knevitt, C., (1987) Community Architecture. Penguin books. LONDON.

4. Acheson, E.D. (1988) Public Health in England – The Report of the Committee of Enquiry into the Future Development of the Public Health Function in England. (Cmnd 289. HMSO, LONDON.)

5. Winslow, Charles Edward A. (1920) The Untilled Fields of Public Health. Science 51: 23

6. HMSO. Saving Lives: Our Healthier Nation (1999)

7. The Stationery Office (1999) Independent Inquiry into Inequalities in Health Report. Chairman Sir Donald Acheson. ISBN 0-11-322173-8.

Duncan Memorial Lecture

University of Liverpool
23 November 1999

Yvette Cooper MP
Minister for public health

Dr William Henry Duncan was appointed 150 years ago yet the problems that plagued him then are not very different from those which engage our attention today. In his work in Liverpool, Duncan worried about the spread of tuberculosis; today, after years of vaccination we worry that tuberculosis is being spread again. Duncan worried about the ventilation of churches, chapels and schools; today we worry about the health risks of smoking, and where Duncan strove to promote and improve sanitation, today's public health officials are striving to improve food hygiene. The concern of public health professionals to identify the causes of health inequalities and those related to mortality and morbidity has not wavered in 150 years.

By the time of his retirement in 1863, William Henry Duncan had made an important and lasting contribution to public health by ensuring that issues of public health were tackled with the seriousness that they deserved, and that resources were allocated to public health on the basis of identified priorities.

But in other ways things have changed since Duncan's time: 100 years ago the life expectancy at birth for women in England was 48 and for men 44. Today life expectancy is 80 for women and 75 for men. Over the same period infant mortality has fallen from over one in ten, to six per thousand. Major killers such as cholera and polio are now under control. But for all the progress we have made, the disturbing truth is that some have not benefited from this progress as fast as others. I come new to public health and have a lot to learn, but I would like to discuss some of the things that have struck me as I come into this job. One thing I have learnt has been the gap between rich and poor in our country, and the most troubling aspect of this is that the gap has grown over the last 20 years and is still growing. It is still the case that, at the end of the second millennium, the chances of a long and healthy life depend on what type of job your parents did, where you live or your ethnic background. That is wrong and we the Government pledge to address this issue.

The life expectancy of a man living in Surrey is a startling 11 years longer than that of a man living in Manchester. Mortality rates for babies born in this country are more than twice as high in infants of mothers born in Pakistan as in infants of mothers born in the United Kingdom. The death rate from coronary heart disease is three times higher among unskilled men than it is among professionals. None of this is news – the rich live longer than the poor, the unemployed are more likely to suffer from depression and those living in sub-standard housing are at greater risk of ill health from cold and damp.

Duncan would not have been surprised to find this so, but he would have been troubled to find that the gap had grown over the last 20 years. In the 1970s the death rate was 53 per cent per cent higher among men in social classes IV and V compared to social classes I and II; by the late Eighties that same differential had increased to 68 per cent. The gap has grown further in the Nineties. In 1993 the mortality rate in Liverpool was 23 per cent above that for England. In Manchester the rate was 29 per cent above the English average; by 1997 the mortality rate in England had fallen and the rates in Liverpool and Manchester had also fallen, but not as fast as the rate for England. They are now 30 per cent and 35 per cent higher than the rate for England.

When Sir Douglas Black was commissioned to report on health inequalities by the then Labour government 22 years ago, little could he have known that the grim statistics which he reported would actually worsen in the following decades. In 1980, in the early days of Mrs Thatcher's government, the Black report was quietly buried. Public health was confined to a ghetto and all we heard was of variations in health, heaven forbid that these variations were associated with unemployment, income levels and educational status. Ministers were not even counting on the possibility that such inequalities existed, never mind that they might be caused by poverty, unemployment or bad housing.

It was another 17 years before a new Labour Secretary of State for Health, Frank Dobson, commissioned Sir Donald Acheson, a former Chief Medical Officer at the Department of Health, to undertake a further review of health inequalities. Sir Donald's report was published almost exactly a year ago, on 26 November 1998, and it has had a strong influence on the Government's health strategy, which we published this July in the White Paper, Saving Lives: Our Healthier Nation.

The report was a landmark which placed health and inequalities firmly on the national agenda. It identified the deep-rooted causes of inequality in our society today, the upstream causes like poverty, unemployment, poor housing, low skill levels, poor access to transport and environmental factors. The report also dealt with the so-called downstream causes like smoking, exercise and diet. No one should believe for a minute that the Acheson report was merely the Black report reheated after 20 years on ice. Nor should anyone think that the Government's attempt to address health inequalities is simply picking up where the Labour ministers of years ago left off. While the fundamental inequalities have persistently grown, the form they take and the nature of society in which they are embedded has changed dramatically, as the Acheson report makes clear.

Decades ago in my constituency in Yorkshire, miners were contracting emphysema as they worked on the coalface. By the Eighties and Nineties many of their sons were suffering stress and depression on the dole. For women born in 1970, the daughters of unskilled men were nine times more likely to become teenage mothers than daughters of professionals, but that risk doubled compared to the previous generation. A generation ago pensioners made up the biggest group of people living in poverty, today it is children. Child poverty has tripled in 20 years since 1979. This increase in child poverty is closely tied to the increase in households where no one is in employment. At the same time educational qualifications have become a far more important determinant of a person's chances in life. The health gap between those who leave school at 16 and those who choose to stay on has risen from 40 per cent in the Seventies to 60 per cent in the 1990s. Women now account for half of the workforce. For women with no qualifications, their chance of entering the workforce has now dropped from 59 per cent in 1984 to 52 per cent more recently; however, among women with higher education, participation in the job market has risen from 78 per cent to 86 per cent in the same period.

I would like to pick up on some of the key issues raised in the Acheson report, show how it is driving the thinking right across the Government, and identify some of the challenges we face in the future. It does seem particularly appropriate to talk about health and inequalities in the Duncan Memorial Lecture, as the Duncan Chair of Public Health at this university is occupied by Professor Margaret Whitehead, who has contributed so much to our understanding of health inequalities. Professor Whitehead worked on the Acheson report and is influential in developing government policy. In Liverpool public health has been a major issue for a long time. It has been defended and practised even in times when it has not been taken seriously at a national level. Here the regional development strategy is placing health at the centre with objectives for regeneration. Better health, in addition to bringing so many other benefits to people, also adds significant value to the economic and social life of this region.

Turning to government policy since the last election, a lot of the work has been done by the Social Exclusion Unit, based in the Cabinet Office and reporting directly to the Prime

Minister. It has drawn together strategic groups to work on a number of issues ranging from teenage pregnancies to access to shops on poorer estates. In addition departments right across government are working individually and in partnership on policies which should reduce health inequalities over time. The challenge is to tackle what Acheson described as the upstream causes of ill health, the deep underlying problems like poverty, unemployment and poor education, and the downstream risks such as smoking, poor diet and low uptake of physical exercise by large sections of the population.

For a start the Government aims to raise the income of the worst-off in this society. The most effective way to raise the incomes of families with children is to help their parents into gainful employment. The number of children who are growing up in relatively disadvantaged families has grown threefold over the last 20 years. By 1995 a third of all children, a staggering four million, were living in households with less than half the national average income. Most of these families are out of work. The Government's measures to promote full employment and to help the unemployed into work are essential to tackle health inequalities in the long term. Being in employment will increase the family income; it is also clear that unemployment of itself is related to ill health. For instance, those who are unemployed are twice as likely to suffer from depression as those in work. Hence tackling unemployment will address ill health by raising the family income and by mitigating the magnitude of ill health resulting from unemployment as an independent variable.

That is why the Government is investing £500 million in the New Deal, to help people back into work. The key thing about the New Deal is the focus on the individual, with advisers who can deal with each individual and with the barriers they face in getting jobs, whether it be lack of education, financial problems, health problems or lack of skills, and focusing on their personal interests and needs. Helping to raise the person's employability in this way will give them a better chance of finding work. But it also means working to regenerate parts of the country where the number of jobs does not reflect the local need for employment. This is why we have focused Regional Development Agencies, as well as regeneration directed at local communities and local estates.

Programmes like the New Deal for Communities are boosting incomes for families in need. Another issue for women is childcare: the new national childcare strategy aims to enable parents who want to work to do so, by bringing affordable childcare to every neighbourhood. The parents of children most at risk of poverty are being given the opportunity to return to work to raise the income for their families.

The best way to keep children out of poverty in the next 20 years is to boost their parents' education today. Evidence shows that mechanisms that link the fortunes of parents and children have changed: as educational qualifications have become more important, people with higher education qualifications tend to have higher wages. They are also far less likely to experience long spells of unemployment throughout their working lives. We know that children from disadvantaged families are less likely to succeed in attaining educational qualifications, less likely to stay on at school after the age of 16 and more likely to have problems with literacy and numeracy. Differences in educational attainment start at a very early age, so that by 22 months children in social classes I and II are likely to be some 14 per cent further along the educational developmental scale than those in classes IV and V. So the Government's drive to raise educational standards and to be intolerant of failure in deprived areas reflects the importance it places on good education. The policies to increase the number of those continuing with education after the age of 16 and wider access to higher education for low-income families should help bring better opportunities for children whose parents did not have these opportunities.

In particular I would like to mention Sure Start; this is a new programme which has not yet had the attention it deserves. A departmental programme investing £450 million over the next three years, it is for families with children under four years of age in the areas of lowest incomes. The idea is to draw together all the services for under-fours and their families, to provide the service that local parents want. We wish to move away from working on a competitive model where different agencies and areas have to bid for resources. When areas have been identified, they have to draw together a programme in order to receive the resources. The programmes that have been coming forward so far indicate that parents, midwives, health visitors, community workers, nursery teachers and local authorities are all becoming involved in developing services for families in low-income areas. The first Liverpool Sure Start has been drawn up in West Everton, and Alder Hey Children's Hospital is closely involved. Sure Start provides a huge opportunity to tackle disadvantage early in children's lives. A lot of resources are going into it and I believe that Sure Start programmes will be most successful where they are deep-rooted in the local community. Programmes that address the needs of the community, that reflect the things that parents want, that neighbours want, rather than programmes drawn up by local professionals, stand a greater chance of delivering the desired outcomes. Whether it is New Deal for Communities, Sure Start or all kinds of regeneration projects, we have to make sure they are geared to what local people want.

In addition to help with education and employment, the Government is taking further action to tackle low income. The decision, for example, to increase child benefit and income support premiums for under-11s will put more cash into the pockets of families with young children. The recently introduced Working Families Tax Credit guarantees working families with dependant children a minimum income of £200 per week. The

Working Families Tax Credit makes a great difference to many families on low income by increasing their income by up to £2,000 a year. These families will actually get the money in their hands.

By the end of this Parliament all of these measures to help low income families should have removed one million children from poverty. This still means, however, that child poverty will continue to be a major challenge. We are aware of that and the Government has set a target for abolishing child poverty altogether over the next 20 years. This is an ambitious target, and in order to reduce child poverty in 20 years, we must start to tackle problems faced by the previous generation right now. As well as giving more help to families with young children, the Government is also boosting the income of the poorest pensioners by bringing in a minimum pension guarantee, so that no pensioner's income falls below £78 per week. And for pensioners in particular, poorly heated houses can be bad for their health. Given the amount of time people spend in their homes, the quality of housing has an impact on health. Acheson said that shelter is an important prerequisite for good health. The most important risk to health is cold and damp, which causes all sorts of illnesses including respiratory diseases. The condition of housing in the country is variable, there are about one-and-a-half million dwellings in England that fall short of the current housing fitness standards laid down in legislation, and in a typical winter there will be two-and-a-half million homes cold enough to cause ill health.

We are also trying to tackle fuel poverty with a new scheme to promote energy efficiency, by cutting the Value Added Tax on domestic fuel and by giving every pensioner household a £100 winter fuel allowance. We are also making additional investment in services to meet the needs of homeless people, including those sleeping rough and those with mental health problems. Additional policies to improve public transport, to cut crime and to improve the environment should help in the long term to improve public health.

The Government plans not only to tackle the upstream causes of ill health and inequalities, but to take action on downstream causes too. This means action in traditional areas such as smoking, diet and physical exercise. However we need to ensure that when addressing these areas, we are conscious of the link between each of these areas and health inequalities. In 1996 29 per cent of men and 28 per cent of women smoked; this ranged from 12 per cent of men and 11 per cent of women in professional occupations to 41 per cent of men and 36 per cent of women in unskilled manual occupations. Even among those who smoked, those in professional occupations smoked less each day than those in unskilled manual occupations. That is why our campaign to reduce death and disease caused by smoking and tobacco is actually a policy for reducing health inequalities as well.

We have comprehensive policies to address the downstream causes. For instance, we have banned tobacco advertising, introduced health education programmes on the dangers of smoking and we plan to provide additional help through smoking cessation clinics and nicotine replacement therapy. We provide these services because 70 per cent of smokers say they want to give up smoking. These measures will also play their part in tackling health inequalities. On food we know, for example, that low intake of certain vegetables can increase the risk of certain cancers including cancer of the colon and rectum. There is evidence that a high intake of salt can lead to high blood pressure while a high intake of fat can lead to heart disease. People on lower incomes are more likely than others to have diets that have a detrimental effect on their health. This is often due to the fact that they are not close enough to shops that sell nutritious food at prices they can afford. They do not have cars to take them to the supermarket so that they can bring all their shopping back in one go. That is why the Social Exclusion Unit has been working on policies to improve access to nutritious food and to tackle the problems in areas without access to affordable high-quality food. These proposals will be launched for consultation shortly.

Some people have suggested that the proper home for public health should not be in the Department of Health but in the Cabinet Office. The argument is that because the cause of public health rests across government, the necessary co-ordination of action would be better achieved by the Cabinet Office. I find this a very interesting suggestion, not least because of the two opposing groups who make it: on the one hand the medical traditionalists who focus on high-technology medical treatments, and on the other hand the public health purists who think that a minister for public health might be distracted if she is in the Department of Health. The latter group expresses the fear that the minister might be sucked into the focus on tangible medical treatments and related issues; they wish instead to move me to the Cabinet Office where the doctors and nurses cannot get at me and distract me from the wider causes of ill health. That would be a huge mistake. To slice public health out of the Department of Health would be a retrograde step that treats public health as an appendage rather than as a mainstream priority which should flood the entire Department. Instead I believe that the values and priorities of public health in tackling health inequalities and the deep-rooted causes of ill health should enable the Department to permeate the entire NHS with them. That is what this Government intends to do.

For a start, delivering a public health agenda requires action right across the NHS. Each health authority in association with other local players, including local authorities, is already required to produce a Health Improvement Programme (HImP) which translates national targets locally. I have already received health improvement programmes from several people, including from Liverpool. One of the main areas which health authorities have been asked to look at is health inequalities, including access to care; we made this very clear in the national guidelines. Also Primary Care Groups have a vital role to play in promoting public health, whether it is to help people give up smoking or by working with Health Action Zones, all of these are ways of improving access to health care which people may not otherwise receive.

This is not just about using the NHS to deliver a public health agenda. It is also about taking the values and priorities that preserve public health right into the heart of the NHS. What has often been referred to as the inverse care law still applies in many areas, where the availability of healthcare does not always match the level of need in that area. Affluent areas are often well served by primary care services, while the more needy and deprived areas struggle to get the basic services they need. It is a sad fact that the areas with most ill health still tend to experience the least satisfactory access to the full range of services. This is illustrated by the fact that the highest rate for heart operations is not in the areas with highest prevalence of heart disease, and further by the fact that people in poor areas are less likely to survive cancer than people in more affluent areas. That is unacceptable. In fact, by putting cancer and heart disease at the top of the Government's priorities we will also be taking on some of the most serious health inequalities. The new cancer director Mike Richards has been charged with assessing the variations in survival rates following the onset of cancer and drawing up a strategy to tackle this problem. We also plan a similar strategy for coronary heart disease. It is the first time that a policy on these two major diseases will be drawn together under one minister and a single team.

It is worth making one final observation. All the words about tackling health inequalities and the causes of health inequalities and ill health would be of no use unless we could deliver results. We need to be very hard-headed about what works and what makes a difference. Campaigns which serve to only make the healthy healthier and to widen the health gap have not done all we have asked of them, and we have had plenty of those in the past. We have made it very clear that we need an evidence-based approach to public health and to tackling inequalities, and that is why the new Health Development Agency, which replaces the Health Education Authority, will be charged with assessing what works. This will ensure that we focus the resources where they can make the most difference to the health inequalities we loathe so much. This is an area where the academic community has a major role to play in assessing the public health polices which can make a difference; they can inform us of timescales over which these policies take effect.

I have attempted during this lecture to show what can be done. This is a huge challenge and we are aware that this is just the start. There will be people who think that there are other more important things that should be put at the top of our agenda, things that they want us to do over the next few years, and we are very keen to hear what they are. In practice the delivery of all these improvements will depend on partnerships between agencies, on the expertise of public health professionals and others right across to local communities. We are very keen to work with you and learn from you about what works.